The

Spirituality

of

Jesus

Nine Disciplines Christ Modeled for Us

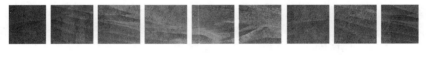

LESLIE T. HARDIN

Kregel
Publications

The Spirituality of Jesus: Nine Disciplines Christ Modeled for Us

© 2009 by Leslie T. Hardin

All rights reserved. No part of this book may be reproduced, stored in a retrieval system, or transmitted in any form or by any means—electronic, mechanical, photocopy, recording, or otherwise—without written permission of the publisher, except for brief quotations in printed reviews.

All Scripture quotations, unless otherwise indicated, are from the *Holy Bible, New International Version®*. Copyright © 1973, 1978, 1984 by International Bible Society. Used by permission of Zondervan. All rights reserved.

Scripture quotations marked KJV are from the King James Version.

Scripture quotations marked NASB are from the NEW AMERICAN STANDARD BIBLE®. Copyright © 1960, 1962, 1963, 1968, 1971, 1972, 1973, 1975, 1977 by The Lockman Foundation. Used by permission. (www.Lockman.org)

Library of Congress Cataloging-in-Publication Data
Hardin, Leslie T.
  The spirituality of Jesus : nine disciplines Christ modeled for us / Leslie T. Hardin.
    p.   cm.
Includes bibliographical references.
1. Jesus Christ—Example. 2. Spirituality. 3. Spiritual life—Christianity. 4. Christian life. I. Title.
BT304.2.H36   2009   248.4—dc22   2009022086

ISBN 978-0-8254-2905-7

Printed in the United States of America

09 10 11 12 13 / 5 4 3 2 1

The

Spirituality

of

Jesus

For my wife,
Kara,
the most spiritual
(as defined in this book)
person I know

Contents

■

Acknowledgments

■

THERE ARE A NUMBER OF PEOPLE I must thank at this point, for without them this book would not exist. My thanks go out to Jim Weaver and the good folks at Kregel for taking a chance on this project. They have challenged me in a gracious and loving manner at every step along the way. Thanks also to Jack Kragt for putting me in touch with them. Without his intervention the proposal would still be searching for a hearing.

Several of my colleagues deserve mention for helping me with the manuscript at several points. David Peters, Robert Ritchie, and Brian Smith read select chapters and provided helpful guidance about how to make my case without alienating half my audience. Garrett Thompson graciously shared some of his research, even though he knew it was for a project he wouldn't get credit for. I credit him now, not just for his notes, but also for his humility and friendship. Acknowledgment and gratitude to the administration at Florida Christian College are also in order, for allowing me to set aside important extracurricular activities to work on this project. Finally, Twila Sias, professor of education at Florida Christian College, has provided the necessary encouragement for me to continue working on this project. From the first time I described the project to her, she has been excited about its use, not just in her discipleship groups and Sunday school classes, but also in her own personal development. She has been to me, in every sense of the word, pastoral.

Dr. Jim Estep of Lincoln Christian College and Seminary has been a great source of encouragement to me during the writing of this book. His expertise in first-century education and willingness to point me to the right resources provided the foundation for discussion of Jesus' childhood education in the Scriptures. Without his help, this book would have less credibility in that area. He also has taken a keen interest in my emergence as an author at a time when I questioned whether this was God's direction for my ministry. I am honored to have his help and privileged to call him a friend.

There are others who have probably been just as helpful whom I have forgotten to mention. Their names have not been omitted intentionally from spite but accidentally from absentmindedness.

All quotations from Scripture are taken from the New International Version, unless otherwise noted. To enhance readability, most Scripture references appear in the endnotes. I have shied away from quoting other translations, not because I question their validity, but for consistency and clarification. I have kept the citations from the original Greek and Hebrew to a minimum, using them only when necessary to keep the argument flowing in a credible way. My intended audience was never the scholarly community but rather the everyday believer searching for answers to the question, How can I be spiritual like Jesus? Therefore, I have tried to keep technical jargon to a minimum and the translation consistent.

I dedicate this book to my wife, Kara. She is a faithful wife, a loving parent, and, above all, a godly woman. I see a legacy in her future akin to that of Susanna Wesley and Grandma Creamer (who, at the time of her death, had over twenty children, grandchildren, and relatives in the ministry). Most authors mention the patience of their wives during the composition of the manuscript, citing long hours at the office and personal time stolen from family cohesion to complete the project. I never understood how it could be so personal to them until now. Kara, thank you for your patience, for letting me be preoccupied with this project, for encouraging me through the doubt, for not nagging me when I spent nights in my office writing, for offering helpful comments about the manuscript, and for your partnership in training our children to be godly.

■

What Is "Spiritual"?

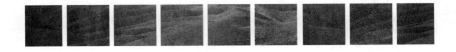

■ ONE OF THE MOST INTERESTING BOOKS I ever encountered bridging New Testament studies and spiritual formation was Stephen Barton's *The Spirituality of the Gospels*. Now out of print, Barton's approach was similar to most critical studies of the Gospels, seeking to identify, not so much the history contained in them, but the emphasis that each writer attempted to convey by the way he arranged the material. However, whereas other critical studies note Matthew's emphasis upon Jesus' teaching (thereby portraying Jesus as a teacher), Barton attempted to uncover the expression of spirituality that each evangelist felt was important. Matthew portrayed a spirituality of obedience to the master's commands. Mark's emphasis upon a "dark, strenuous spirituality"[1] was born from an attempt to encourage a community undergoing persecution. In Barton's view, Luke-Acts is concerned with the presence of the Spirit of God and the joy found in Christ, and John with an interpersonal relationship with Jesus, which is available to his disciples and resembles the close dependence he had upon his Father. What I found most interesting about Barton's approach was that there was no consideration of the spirituality of Jesus himself, only that of the Gospel writers.

I made the same disappointing discovery when I picked up the classic *The Study of Spirituality*. This work is a thorough and detailed compendium of spirituality throughout the centuries and is highly recommended for study of this kind. The work explores spirituality from the Old Testament era to that of the modern American church and covers various expressions of spirituality in the modern church. After perusing the chapter on the spirituality of the Old Testament, I quickly turned the page to uncover what Cheslyn Jones might say regarding the spirituality of Jesus. What I found was a chapter based on the same methodology—the spirituality of the Gospel writers. The chapter, simply titled "The New Testament," quickly moves from the spirituality of the Evangelists to the spirituality of Paul and John.[2] Still puzzling to me was the avoidance of any consideration of Jesus' spirituality. Modern biblical studies lean toward the conclusion that more information can be gleaned from the Gospels regarding the intention of the authors (i.e., Mark or Luke) than the first-century Jew, Jesus of Nazareth. Albert Schweitzer's summation that "there is nothing more negative than the result of the critical study of the Life of Jesus" still seems applicable.[3]

So that got me to thinking. What if we took the Gospels at face value and attempted to uncover the spirituality of Jesus? What if the Gospels, instead of *only* presenting a theological argument about Jesus, also accurately portrayed the disciplines in which Jesus was engaged? What could we learn about Jesus and his spirituality from an accurate portrayal of his life and ministry in the Gospels? It's a question that deserves attention, but it has largely been ignored by both history and theology. It is a question that must be governed by historical investigation and then set in proper theological context. It's the question that drives this book: Was Jesus spiritual?

Was Jesus "Spiritual"?

It sounds like a ridiculous question, doesn't it? Of course he was spiritual! The Gospels tell us that he demonstrated the power of the Spirit in his life by casting out demons, quieting the waves, healing those with incurable physical ailments, and being "transfigured" in the presence of three of his closest disciples. These are obvious signs that the Spirit of God was at work in him. The Gospels also exhibit Jesus' total dependence upon his Father (what scholars sometimes call a "God-consciousness"), a recognition that he needed God in his life at every moment. He considered doing God's will more important than eating, sleeping, and having a place to live. His "food" was to do the will of the one who sent him.[4] No one would argue that Jesus wasn't dependent upon his Father or that the Spirit of God wasn't at work in him. If the flowing of the Spirit of God in a person's life is what makes a person "spiritual," Jesus certainly qualifies. Peter preached that "God anointed Jesus of Nazareth with the Holy Spirit and power" (Acts 10:38), and Jesus' own testimony was that the Spirit of God was upon him.[5]

The question of Jesus' spirituality needs further clarification. Was Jesus *made* spiritual? Does his siring by the Holy Spirit automatically give him a proclivity for performing miracles? Was his God-consciousness downloaded *Matrix*-style into his brain at his baptism? Or were there spiritual *activities* that Jesus engaged in on a regular basis that allowed the Spirit free reign in his life? Luke tells us on two separate occasions that Jesus "grew," and not just in his physical attributes. As Luke parallels the miraculous conception, birth, growth, and ministries of John the Baptist and Jesus, he makes it clear that both of them *developed* spiritually. John the Baptist "grew and became strong in spirit" (Luke 1:80) while Jesus "grew and became strong" (2:40), particularly "in wisdom and stature, and in favor with God and men" (2:52). That he grew in "wisdom" and "favor with God" suggests that there was an aspect of his development, at least during his childhood and adolescence, which required guidance, assistance, prodding, and the formation of godly habits. The verb Luke uses for "grew" is in the imperfect tense, denoting that his growth was continuous and ongoing, not a onetime event.

This is a far cry from some of the early portraits of Jesus that emerged in the second and third centuries. As the popularity of the four canonical gospels grew, other "gospels" (i.e., lives of Jesus) appeared, purporting to fill in the story of Jesus' childhood untold by Matthew and Luke, particularly the events of his early childhood. Stories about Jesus' miraculous God-knowledge are common to these documents and had to be dealt with. One example is the *Infancy Gospel of Thomas*, which claims that Jesus bested his teachers at every turn during his early childhood. On one occasion, Jesus was annoyed at having to learn the Greek and Hebrew alphabets (apparently he already knew them) and asked his teacher to explain to him the value of the letters. When the teacher could not, the child Jesus cursed him to death. Jesus' next teacher was not so quick to challenge him! Instead, his flattery of Jesus' intelligence motivated the child to raise to life the teacher he had cursed.[6] These are just two examples of the kinds of stories told about Jesus in this type of literature. They tell of a messianic child who could do miracles from his childhood, often with little or no discretion about how to control his emotions and use those miraculous powers for honorable purposes, rather than from whim or spite.

These pseudo-gospels tell a story of Jesus that is at utter variance with the New Testament witness that his spirituality was *developed* through regular habits that afforded opportunity for the Spirit to flow through him. His parents regularly took him to Jerusalem for the corporate worship feasts, and he continued that practice until the time of his death.[7] He was a student of Scripture and was able to cite texts from memory, suggesting more than a casual acquaintance with God's Word. Prayer and solitude were necessary for him, not just to spend time with the Father, but also to cast down temptation,[8] to ask for direction on the choosing of the Twelve,[9] and to prepare for the climax of his ministry.[10] Even sharing meals with the outcasts, the poor, and on occasion the Pharisees created opportunities for dialogue about life in the kingdom.[11] Jesus regularly engaged in activities that both fostered and allowed the Spirit of God to flow through him and prepare him for opportunities to share with those around him what it means to be godly, Spirit-filled, kingdom-minded . . . spiritual.

The Nature of Spiritual Formation

At the heart of our inquiry is what we mean when we say "spiritual." For some, spirituality happens in ecstatic experiences like emotional worship, speaking in tongues, new revelations, or miraculous events. Among other things, the early charismatic movement was characterized by inclusion of dreams and visions in both private and public expression and confidence in God's leading through the ecstatic elements in much the same way that Word-centered Protestants find God's voice in the text of Scripture.[12] Modern American Christianity places great value and trust in the "big event," the spiritual conference, the rally, the revival, and the concert. If we truly desire our children to study our methods, they are likely to learn that significant kingdom ministry takes place only on a stage before thousands of people.

The classic Christian witness has been that spirituality takes place in the everyday events of life. For Ignatius of Antioch (c. AD 110) the mark of spiritual maturity among believers was made evident in their obedience to the local bishop.[13] François Fénelon (AD 1651–1715), spiritual guide for the family of the Duc de Beauvilleiers (who had eight daughters), warned them against neglecting their daily responsibilities to seek God in the emotionally ecstatic: "You will not get closer to God by neglecting your daily responsibilities and calling it 'spiritual.'"[14] Responding to those who hope to find God in spiritual conferences and ecstatic meetings, Eugene Peterson quips in *The Wisdom of Each Other* that one is "more likely to find a spiritual readiness for the uniqueness of the Christian message among those who are dealing with the basics of daily existence than among those who are trying to escape them."[15] We meet God, not in the hyperemotional experiences that North American Christianity has come to expect, but in the common, everyday stuff of life.

Another question concerns the *work* of spiritual formation. Does God initiate spiritual formation? Some think so. For some, spiritual development is the work of God alone, and nothing we do can affect God's working in us, either positively or negatively.[16] For others, spiritual formation must be cultivated, grown with care and attention like a prized rose garden. Paul suggests that spiritual development takes place as we *partner* with God. He tells the Philippians, "continue to work out your salvation with fear and trembling, for it is God who works in you to will and to act according to his good purpose" (Phil. 2:12–13). It is our responsibility to work out our salvation even as God works in us. Spiritual development, then, is partnership with God. He offers grace freely, and we respond with loving obedience.

John Tyson sums this up well in his introduction to *Invitation to Christian Spirituality*:

We prefer to speak of "being in love" as a mystical experience that bursts upon the horizon of our emotions suddenly and without warning. There is something in the emotive quality of the experience that causes us to refrain from tarnishing the mystery by speaking of it in terms of strategy or our own intentions; perhaps there is also something in the riskiness of love that urges us to leave an escape hatch open (and one without culpability) should love not last. If we fell in love without intention or consideration, it seems reasonable that we could also fall out of love without blame or stigma of failure. This same sort of dilemma in language and conception persists in the popular understanding of Christian Spirituality. We expect a deep and transformative relationship with God to come upon us magically, without planning and preparation, without attending to the means of grace, and without attention to formative disciplines like prayer, scripture study, and self-denial. When this relationship fails to grow beyond the initial stages we are willing to excuse ourselves from culpability since it is by grace, or through the power of the Holy Spirit, that "friendship with God" occurs at all.

This popular, and perhaps subconscious, understanding of spiritual life is at utter variance with the classical Christian witness. The Pauline injunction bears repeating: "Work out your own salvation with fear and trembling; for God is at work in you, both to will and to work for his good pleasure" (Phil. 2:12). The development of Christian Spirituality is a cooperative effort, it involves God's work (the gift of grace) and our work (the faithful response); taken together and intermingled these two works produce transformation, wholeness, and life with God. This means that for spiritual growth to occur many of us will have to become more intentional about Christian Spirituality and spiritual disciplines. We will have to stop thinking of spirituality as something that comes upon us only unbidden and in full bloom. Rather, we will have to recognize (in accordance with the NT analogies) that the life of grace is cultivated, nurtured, and grown over the span of a lifetime.[17]

If, as Tyson proposes, spirituality involves both God's work and ours, it is natural to see how Jesus needed to engage in spiritual activity that produced "wholeness and life with God." This is what I hope to explore in this book.

Spirituality and the Uniqueness of Jesus

It's these everyday matters that I'd like to explore. If spirituality is defined by the miraculous and the ecstatic, then our tendency will be to see Jesus' spirituality in terms of the supernatural works he performed. I believe that Jesus did, in fact, perform these miracles but that he did so as part of his unique role as the Son of God. If raising the dead, healing the genetically blind, and cleansing leprosy in an instant are the marks of spiritual development, then most of us will not qualify. While some of his miracles were repeated in his own ministry, the world generally agrees that the ministry of Jesus of Nazareth was unique among the prophets and holy men of Israel. To take the miraculous events that make his ministry unique and then employ them as the standard of Christian spirituality makes little sense and creates an ideal we can never achieve.

Jesus' spirituality is manifest, not in the miraculous, but rather in the routine activities that garnered partnership with the Spirit, which in turn gave rise to miracles and supernatural events. In short, Jesus' spirituality is seen in the things he did that allowed the Spirit to grow and flow unimpeded in his life. By searching the Gospels, admittedly documents that focus on his miraculous God-power, we catch a glimpse of the spiritual practices that Jesus regularly engaged in. Seeing these in action, we are then able to take the advice of Thomas à Kempis to "let the life of Christ be our guide" as we engage in the study of spirituality.[18] If Jesus' spirituality was fueled by everyday practices, so our spirituality will benefit from engaging in those same disciplines that promote wholeness and intimacy with God.

The Way Forward

Our task in the next several chapters will be to seek out those practices in which Jesus regularly engaged and to consider how they gave free rein for the Spirit to work in and through him. I have identified nine spiritual disciplines evident in Jesus' human existence: prayer and solitude, resisting temptation, Scripture study, corporate worship, submission, simplicity, care for the oppressed and outcast, meal-sharing, and evangelism and proclamation. I hope to explore these as a way of answering the question, What does it mean to be spiritual? We will not only consider Jesus' methodology in these activities but also give thought to how they opened up avenues for the Spirit's manifestation of power.

After we have considered what existed in Jesus' everyday spirituality, we will give pause to consider some of the anachronisms of our study. What is missing from the Gospels' presentation of Jesus' spirituality? What did we expect to find but now seems conspicuously absent? Does that absence mean that it wasn't important to Jesus? Or is the absence of that practice characteristic of the messianic ministry, with the expectation that the practice will resume (or at least take on different form) in the new covenant? Moreover, what benefit does this study have for our understanding of Christian spirituality and the practice of being "spiritual" in the twenty-first century? These are important questions, and we will do our best to make the appropriate application.

Points of Clarification

So far, I've been expressing a desire to explore the *human* side of Jesus' spirituality, to investigate the things he did on a regular basis that fostered intimacy with God and the power of the Spirit. But before we go any further, we must set some boundaries on this discussion, so we don't fall into error. There's a good chance that some of you reading this are concerned at this point, even angered, at the possible direction this study might take. So let's clarify what we're *not* saying before we get started.

Jesus' Spiritual Habits Did Not Make Him Divine

There's a chance that you're reading this and thinking, "Is he saying that Jesus did these things, and that by doing them he became the Son of God? Did Jesus *become* God by being so spiritual?" Absolutely not. The clear testimony of Scripture is that Jesus was divine before his birth. John tells us that he was "in the beginning . . . with God" and in fact "was God" (John 1:1). Jesus had a role in creation,[19] proving his divinity before his incarnation. He existed in the beginning with God, and to suggest that he did anything in his ministry or life to create divinity within himself brings us dangerously close to both Gnosticism (an error of the second century that focused on the growth of the "spark of divinity within" all of us) and adoptionism (a belief that God adopted the man Jesus as his son because of Jesus' holiness and obedience). Both of these errors were cast down by the early church fathers. Even before Jesus' conception, the angel told Mary, "He will be great and will be called the Son of the Most High" (Luke 1:32).

Understanding the relationship between his humanity and his divinity has been difficult for the church since the beginning. Early church history is filled with controversies over the exact relationship between Jesus' human existence and his divine nature. More than a few councils resulted in numerous creeds (official statements) attempting to articulate exactly how we should think responsibly about this dual nature. The consensus has been that according to the New Testament witness, Jesus was both fully God and fully man. While he was "God the One and Only, who is at the Father's side" (John 1:18), "he too shared in their humanity" and was "made like his brothers in every way" (Heb. 2:14, 17). It's this humanity that I hope to explore, without neglecting Jesus' divine nature and without suggesting that his spirituality made him divine.

Jesus Did Not "Channel" the Spirit

In paganism and witchcraft one gains access to the spiritual forces of nature (and even those beyond nature) by performing chants and mantras. These "spells" are supposed to call forth the spirits and subject them to the will of the mediator. This view is not unlike that of Morton Smith, who believed that Jesus was nothing more than a first-century Jewish magician, who taught people how to channel the Spirit of God in ways that would ward off evil spirits and destructive curses. In his view, Jesus' use of God's name, at least in cases of exorcism, "enabled the magician to call effectively for the god to come and enforce his orders."[20]

To think that Jesus is "channeling" the Spirit, calling the Spirit of God into his life by his prayer, fasting, solitude, and other disciplines is to stray far from the testimony of Scripture. The only time we see the Spirit descending on Jesus is at his baptism,[21] and from that point forward there is no hint or suggestion that Jesus ever either (1) lost the Spirit and had to call him forth or (2) forced the Spirit to do his bidding. He was in constant submission to the Father (John 5:16–23) and was not "channeling" the Spirit.

What, then, is the relationship between his divinity, his humanity, and his spirituality? I believe that Jesus was in every way the substance, the representation, the "icon" of God.[22] I also believe that Jesus was, on more than one occasion, tempted to either forsake his divine nature or use it for selfish purposes.[23] If it were not possible to forsake his divine status (or at least misuse it), then the temptation means nothing. Why tempt someone who is impervious to temptation? The fact that Satan attempted it suggests that he reckoned it a possibility. Jesus' spirituality, then, seems to have served several purposes. First, by engaging in practices like prayer, solitude, and submission, he drew strength from the Spirit to overcome temptation. We will see in a later chapter that the wilderness experience immediately following his baptism was not the only time Jesus was tempted. Second, some of Jesus' habits of spiritual devotion put him in a position to be *used* in meaningful ways by the Spirit. Having fellowship meals with the outcasts and attending to the major feasts put him in positions where the Spirit could lead him to say the right thing to the right people in just the right way. Third, Jesus' practice of spirituality was a matter of responsible maintenance of the Spirit's presence in his life. That he studied and memorized the Scriptures shows that he wasn't willing simply to walk into situations unprepared, hoping that the Spirit would miraculously lead him. The Spirit was active in his life, and some of his spiritual habits created the human conditions necessary to allow the Spirit free rein.

This does not mean that I have worked out the proper relationship between his divinity, humanity, and spirituality. I suspect that they will always have to be in balance and that, like the early church, we will have to work hard to ensure that we've thought about the subject correctly and that we haven't gone astray while trying to articulate it.

Jesus Did Not Do These Things for Himself

There is a real danger in a study like this to begin to ask questions like, If Jesus was fully God, was he praying to himself? or, When he went to the synagogue, was he worshiping himself? These questions are not irrelevant, but they take us away from the classic witness of the New Testament that, while Jesus, the Spirit, and the Father are distinctly one in nature, they are also distinctly three separate entities, or persons, of the Godhead. The descriptions of Jesus' baptism in the Synoptic Gospels tell us that as Jesus was coming up out of the water, the Spirit was descending on him, and the Father was speaking from heaven.[24] That Jesus was performing his ministry and duties on earth does not mean that the throne of heaven sat empty. One of the major features of John's gospel is Jesus' dependence upon and submission to his Father. Over one hundred times in John's gospel Jesus has something to say about the "Father."[25] Jesus also says that when he ascends to heaven he will send the Spirit to continue his work.[26] During his ministry Jesus demonstrated his distinctness from both the Father and the Spirit. To suggest that Jesus prays to himself, worships himself, or even submits to himself goes beyond the teaching of the New Testament.

With these clarifications, our inquiry can both enjoy its proper freedom and be prevented from going too far.

For Further Reflection

1. What does it mean, in your view, to be "spiritual"?
2. In what way was Jesus' spirituality a pattern for all believers?
3. In what way was Jesus' spirituality unique to his role as Messiah, as Son of God?
4. What is the relationship between Jesus and the Spirit of God?

ONE

■

Prayer and Solitude

PRAYER OFTEN SEEMS LIKE A DEEP MYSTERY. Judging by the number of books that have appeared in Christian history on the subject of prayer, it is apparently easier explained than practiced. There are many questions that Christians ask about prayer in general: When I pray, what do I say? Is there an appropriate posture? Is there a more respectful tone that I should use when praying? Are there particular words that are more effective than others? Should I pray one set prayer repetitively, or is it better to pray free expressions of the soul? Then there are the special circumstances: How do I pray for a sick loved one? What do I ask for? What if I am the one suffering? How do I express my anger toward God without invoking his wrath?

I first learned to pray in the context of family and worship, and my tutoring fell on two extremes. On the one end were the prayers of my grandfather, Leslie Ewell Clinkenbeard. He was a man steeped in the King James Bible, and when he prayed he addressed God as "Thee" and "Thou." It wasn't that he felt that those words were more effective than modern English, but simply that when he thought of God, King James terminology came to the front of his mind. Listening to him pray (either at the Communion table or over dinner) was a high and holy event, for he was sincere and greatly respectful. On the other end of my training was the counsel of my youth leaders and camp counselors, who assured me that God was *not* impressed with Victorian English and that I should just pour out my heart and mind to him. "God wants to spend time with you, and he just wants you to say whatever is in your heart and mind." As I matured, I realized that not everything in the depths of my heart and mind should be expressed in the presence of the Almighty.

As we examine the prayer life of Jesus, we see that while he was free to pour out his most intense emotions ("My soul is overwhelmed with sorrow to the point of death"; Matt. 26:38), he remained immensely respectful ("Yet not as I will, but as you will"; Matt. 26:39). Perhaps, rather than thinking of this in terms of two extremes, we can think about prayer, along with the twentieth-century theologian Karl Barth, as a quest, a journey toward God to ask him for strength and courage to help us be obedient to his will.[1] The Gospels portray Jesus in just this way. Granted, his "journey" toward the Father was not the same as ours, for he was "the one who came from heaven" (John 3:13), and his communication with the Father was not about his seeking salvation but about keeping open the conduit of the Spirit. For Jesus prayer was an opportunity to connect with the power of the Spirit, to be alone with the Father, to seek God's counsel and guidance on important ministry matters, and to seek strength and courage to be obedient to the Father's will when tempted. It's no surprise to anyone familiar with the Gospels that Jesus spent much time in prayer. What may come as a shock to modern readers of the Gospels, however, is the amount of time Jesus spent in prayer. Whereas modern Western Christians are accustomed to blocking out, for example, fifteen to twenty minutes for prayer, this time is negligible by Jesus' standards. He spent hours in prayer, sometimes nights, and his teaching reflected his own personal practice: prayer—both private and public—is simple, honest communication with the Father about real-life struggles.

Praying in Private

The most striking aspect of Jesus' prayer life was the amount of time he spent praying alone. Jesus often retreated from the crowds to be alone with his disciples. After a long teaching opportunity on the Sea of Galilee, he left the crowds and went back into the house with his disciples, where he continued to teach them privately.[2] John tells us that Jesus was careful not to entrust himself too intimately to the crowds for fear of their dependence upon a miraculous brand of spirituality.[3] Jesus' practice of withdrawing from the crowds has suggested to some that he was an introvert, needing to recharge his physical and emotional batteries by spending time alone.[4]

Jesus' practice of withdrawal, however, was less about his temperament and more about spending time with his Father. As the news of his healing ministry spread, the crowds relentlessly pursued him for help with sickness and ailments. Luke tells us that "Jesus often withdrew to lonely places and prayed" (Luke 5:16). Private prayer preceded the question to his disciples, "Who do the crowds say I am?" (Luke 9:18); and eight days later Jesus took three of his disciples—Peter, James, and John—up the mountain with him where the Transfiguration occurred "as he was praying" (Luke 9:28–29). These times alone in prayer gave Jesus pause to consider, not only the will of his Father, but also the reaction of the crowds and their true motives. Jesus taught his disciples from the depths of his own experience that we should spend less time praying to be seen and more time praying in the closet with the door shut.[5]

The time of prayer seemed less important for him than the practice itself, for Jesus can be found praying both early in the morning and late at night. After a long day of teaching and confrontation in the synagogue, Jesus and his disciples immediately left the synagogue and went to the home of Peter to heal his mother-in-law. That evening, the crowd brought to Jesus those who needed healing, and he ministered to them until well after sunset. Nevertheless, he was found very early the next morning, before sunrise, praying—praying so long, in fact, that more than a few people began looking for him.[6] After the feeding of the five thousand men, Jesus sent his disciples ahead of him to the north side of the Sea of Galilee while he went alone into the mountainous country to pray. It was about the fourth watch of the night (3–6 A.M.) when Jesus finally caught up with them on the water.[7] Since he sent the crowds and disciples away around dusk (Mark 6:47, "when evening came"), he must have spent several hours in prayer before catching up to them. Before Jesus chose the Twelve to be his disciples, Luke says that he "spent the night praying to God" (Luke 6:12). Jesus often can be found in the pages of Scripture withdrawing from the crowds to spend time in prayer, asking the Father for guidance on matters related to his ministry.

On several occasions we find Jesus retreating from the crowds simply to be alone. But the evidence suggests that he was doing more than simply seeking a little peace and quiet. Instead, we find him withdrawing from the busyness of his ministry to *be alone with God*. This is the classic definition of solitude—not being alone, but withdrawing from the everyday stuff of life to be alone with the Father. Did this time alone restore his energy? Probably, but not in a way that being alone refuels the normal introvert. We might be able to say that if Jesus had simply withdrawn without praying. The fact that he spent these times alone *in prayer* suggests that a spiritual rejuvenation necessary to continue his work of ministry was taking place.

Praying the Ordinary

Leafing through the pages of the Gospels, looking for evidence of Jesus' routine spirituality, we find the content of his prayers very ordinary, lacking an overtly ethereal and supernatural tone. Some of his prayers were (in the classic sense of the word) mundane, pertaining to the stuff of everyday life. They were simple, and his teaching on prayer reflects the simplicity that he practiced and passed on to his disciples.

Every young Jewish child was taught to say the Shema (Deut. 6:4–6) as part of a regimen of prayer. Jewish parents taught their children to recite twice daily, "Hear, O Israel: The LORD our God, the LORD is one."[8] Remarking on Jesus' godly upbringing, Luke says that he "grew . . . in favor with God" (Luke 2:52), suggesting a growing familiarity with the Jewish forms of ceremonial and liturgical prayer. Jesus gave thanks for meals before he ate[9] and praised the Father for simple things for which he was grateful.[10] The Gospels present Jesus as the host, the patriarch, presiding over the Passover Feast, which required him to recite a number of ceremonial prayers connected to the liturgy of the Passover.[11] And yet, in some way, listening to him pray was inspiring, for the disciples once heard him pray and asked him to teach them to pray as he did.[12]

Much of Jesus' teaching about prayer is concerned less with liturgical forms pregnant with theological jargon, and more about honest, simple communication with the Father. He taught his followers what is now called the Lord's Prayer.[13] We have no evidence that Jesus ever prayed this particular form—rather, the author of Hebrews tells us that Jesus was "without sin" (4:15), so it makes little sense to believe that Jesus prayed the part about asking for forgiveness—but we can easily see the simple themes from which the prayer is composed. He addressed his holy Father, prayed for the reign of God's kingdom here on earth, and asked for a little bit of food and the strength to overcome temptation. He taught his disciples to pray this way, articulating simple, yet profound themes prominent in his teaching ministry. They were not to babble like the pagans[14] but were to use plain, honest speech, presenting their requests to God in humble and dignified fashion. "The God who can stir up new languages at Babel is not impressed with elo-quence."[15] If we find Jesus teaching his disciples to pray in simple, uncomplicated, non-repetitive patterns, we can assume that Jesus prayed this way also.

Jesus spent time teaching his disciples *not* to pray like the reli-gious leaders of his day. Their propensity for self-righteous display and long, showy prayers caused Jesus great consternation, enough, in fact, that he said that they "for a show make lengthy prayers" (Mark 12:40). He once told a parable about a Pharisee who stood on the street corner, praising God above that he was nothing like the tax collector. In the parable, the tax collector's prayer consisted of a single sentence: "God, have mercy on me, a sinner" (Luke 18:9–14). Jesus' aggravation with the showy prayer practices of the Pharisees demonstrates a chasm between his own habits and the Pharisaic tendencies he wanted to caution his disciples about.

Two parables that Jesus told about prayer are commonly mis-understood: the parable of the unjust judge and the parable of the friend at midnight.[16] In the first parable Jesus tells of a judge who "neither feared God nor cared about men" (Luke 18:2, 4). A widow, seeking justice, kept coming to him with no success. The judge eventually got tired of her repetitive request and granted her justice. This parable was told so that the disciples "should always pray and not give up" (18:1), but the reason was *not* focused upon the widow's persistence. The parable does not suggest that God is the judge and that our persistent requests presented before him will eventually be granted. Rather, Jesus explicitly calls the judge "unjust" (18:6), a quality wholly opposite from God's character. The parable is told in the negative: "God is not like this." God is not like the judge, who will not listen to a cry for help. He is always listening, and, unlike the judge, "will see that they get justice, and quickly" (18:8). The parable of the friend at midnight works in much the same way, suggesting that even though friends are reluctant to help rude neighbors in the middle of the night, God is not like this. No request brought to him is unheard and (if I may loosely paraphrase the point) "he will see that they get bread, and quickly."

Asking for Guidance

On a few occasions we find Jesus praying for guidance, asking for the Father's direction. Mark tells us that Jesus once got up very early in the morning to spend time alone in prayer. When Peter found him, Jesus' response to the pressing crowds was to say, "Let us go somewhere else—to the nearby villages—so I can preach" (Mark 1:35–39). Was Jesus seeking guidance from his Father about whether or not to stay in that location and, if not, where to travel next? A more ambiguous text is Luke 3:21–22, which states that immediately after his baptism, as Jesus was praying, heaven opened up and the Spirit descended upon Jesus. What was Jesus praying for at his baptism?

A clearer example of Jesus' prayer for guidance takes place in conjunction with the selection of the Twelve. The night before he chose the Twelve, he spent the night in prayer. This can be seen clearly in Luke 6:12, but the full story is apparent only when we piece together all four gospel accounts. Jesus went through the cities and towns of Galilee preaching the good news of the kingdom. Seeing that the people needed direction and guidance, he asked them to pray for workers: "Ask the Lord of the harvest, therefore, to send out workers into his harvest field" (Matt. 9:38). Mark 3:13 tells us that once he asked them to pray, he left them and spent the night in prayer in the mountains. When morning came, he returned to the crowd and chose twelve of them to help him carry on the work of his ministry. We can only assume that Jesus spent this night in prayer asking God for guidance about which men from the crowd were best suited to help him carry on the work of spreading the message of the kingdom.

Interceding for Others

Many times Jesus prayed alone, and if we are not careful we can easily assume that his practice of prayer was completely about himself, asking for guidance, casting down temptation, and submitting himself to the will of his Father. But on occasion Jesus prayed before large crowds. Jesus stood before the crowd of five thousand men (with their accompanying women and children), and later the four thousand, and offered thanks for the bread that was about to be multiplied.[17] Before the raising of Lazarus he prayed "for the benefit of the people standing here" (John 11:41–42). He prayed in the presence of the Twelve often, and this was never more evident than at the Passover meal during his final week.[18]

To be certain, Jesus did spend a considerable amount of time praying for his own wants and needs (what Richard Foster calls "Simple Prayer"[19]). This is not the complete story, however, for we also find Jesus praying for Peter, that the Adversary would not completely destroy him.[20] As he discussed this with Peter, it became clear to Peter that Jesus had *already* spent a considerable amount of time interceding to the Father on his behalf. The crowds on occasion brought their children to Jesus to have him lay his hands on them and pray for them. It was customary to bring young children and infants to rabbis and elders for blessing,[21] and that people brought them to Jesus suggests that he regularly welcomed and prayed for them. Had he turned them away and refused to do so, the Gospels would have made it clear that he did not consider this a valuable or worthwhile endeavor. Instead, the Gospels portray Jesus rebuking this very attitude in his disciples and welcoming the little children who came to him.[22]

The clearest presentation of Jesus' intercession is found in John 17. This prayer takes place in the upper room during Jesus' final Passover. The patriarch of the family normally presided over the ceremony (just as my grandfather always said the official prayer over the Thanksgiving and Christmas meals from the head of the table) and offered a number of liturgical prayers as part of the Passover worship ritual. Jesus deviated from the expected pattern a bit by concluding this meal with his disciples with a lengthy prayer recorded only in John. In this prayer he initially prayed for himself and his coming "glorification" (through suffering—vv. 1–5). But his prayer quickly turned from his coming trial to his disciples. He prayed that they would be unified in their devotion to him upon his departure and that they would remain faithful to him in their own coming trial (vv. 6–19). Jesus then concluded his prayer by interceding for those who would believe as a result of the disciples' ministries (vv. 20–23). Jesus' prayers were not solely about his own wants and desires. The record reveals an intense intercession for those he loved.

Struggling in Prayer

For those who believe strongly in the divinity of Christ, one of the most troubling aspects of his life has to be his struggle in the garden of Gethsemane. The night that he was betrayed and arrested, he left the upper room and went to the Mount of Olives. Jesus had been spending his evenings there,[23] no doubt preparing for this event, creating this space for himself in preparation for his trial. And when that time came, he was found in the place that was comfortable for him.

The struggle is evident first in the *posture* that he takes during this prayer. No other evidence in the Gospels about Jesus' practice of prayer suggests that his posture mattered. But when Jesus comes to the garden the night before his suffering, Mark says that at one point he "fell to the ground" (14:35). Luke tells us that he got on his knees and that when he was finished he "rose from prayer" (22:41, 45) and encouraged to disciples to get up and pray.[24] The agony is further illustrated in Luke's statement that he sweat something like drops of blood in his anguish.[25]

Jesus' distress also can be seen in the *content* of his prayer. Matthew, Mark, and Luke all agree that his prayer consisted of appeals to his Father about the "cup" that he was about to drink.[26] This cup is most likely the cup of wrath described in the Song of the Suffering Servant (Isa. 51:17-23). The song is a long tale of Israel's disobedience, Yahweh's wrath, an obedient servant who suffers on behalf of the people, and the salvation that comes to the entire world (Jew and Gentile alike) because of the Servant's vicarious suffering. Just before the Servant suffers, Isaiah describes God's wrath as a goblet of (blood-colored) wine that must be emptied. The cup was originally poured for Israel, but Yahweh declared that he had "taken out of your [Israel's] hand the cup that made you stagger" and that Israel would never drink from it again (Isa. 51:22). The cup is then poured out, not on Israel, but upon the Servant as he does the will of Yahweh in suffering the cup for Israel.[27] Jesus prayed, on three separate occasions, "Let this cup pass from me" (Matt. 26:39, 42, 44; Mark 14:35-36, 39, 41). The Gospels are clear at every turn, from Jesus' baptism to his resurrection, that Jesus knew his role to be that of the Suffering Servant who would bear the punishment of God's wrath innocently for the nation of Israel and thereby inaugurate a universal salvation.[28] Jesus' struggle in prayer is to accept, now that the hour is upon him, the cup that God had ordained long ago for him to suffer.

To be certain there was a measure of temptation that Jesus was overcoming at Gethsemane. Satan had tempted him before with the allegiance of the world's kingdoms *without* suffering (something we will return to in a later chapter),[29] and it's reasonable to assume that he struggled with the same temptation at this point now that the suffering was actually upon him. He was "made like his brothers in every way" (Heb. 2:17) and knows what it's like to struggle in prayer.

Praying Like Jesus

The evidence from the Gospels reveals that Jesus frequently spent time alone in prayer and that his prayers were simple and honest, not extravagant and mystical. The posture was not important to him, and neither were the words he used. Though he spent time alone, he was not afraid to pray in crowds or before groups of people, and even then his prayers were not designed to impress. He operated from the belief that his Father was listening when he prayed, even if that prayer included the genuine struggle to be obedient to the Father's will. If we were looking for evidence of Jesus' everyday practice in prayer, these are the characteristics that stand out and become worthy of emulation.

Three points of application come to mind as we draw this study to a close.

Jesus Spent Much Time in Prayer

His very life and practice—of spending hours in prayer, not minutes—goes against the grain of the fast-paced culture in which Americans live and work. Our attention to prayer cannot always (and perhaps should not) mimic every aspect of that which Jesus embodied. To spend hours in prayer may be infeasible for some, but there is no doubt that many believers today spend far less time in prayer than is ideal or needed. Jesus' long sessions of prayer make us rethink our own practice in prayer and give us hope that this greater fellowship with the Father is humanly possible if we would only take time to engage him.

Jesus Concentrated on His Relationship with the Father

Books on prayer abound, and often the purpose of them is to teach, as Origen did in the third century, "how to pray and what to pray for."[30] Jesus was less concerned with the ritual of prayer (the form, the wording, even the tone) than he was with the relationship he was building with his Father. Though he prayed the liturgical prayers during the Passover meal and was no doubt graceful as he offered up public prayers, his practice and teaching regarding prayer hint away from prescripted formulas and meaningless platitudes. His prayers reveal a deep, intimate relationship with God that sprang from countless hours in fellowship, pouring out his heart and listening in response. We would do well to imitate him in this, casting off theologically expected vocabulary and simply being genuine (yet always respectful) with the Father in prayer.

Jesus' Struggle in Prayer Gives Us Hope

As we struggle to be obedient to the will of God, so too our Brother struggled to become obedient to the path the Father had set before him. His angst in the garden speaks volumes to our own souls, which so easily turn away. When we struggle to obey, we have assurance that even Jesus struggled to be obedient. That he overcame the temptation and remained faithful is also an encouragement. The author of Hebrews says that "he learned obedience from what he suffered" (5:8). No matter how difficult the current task, in prayer there is always hope and strength available. God granted Jesus the strength necessary to do his will, and he will do the same for us so that we also might be faithful.

For Further Reflection

1. How much time do you regularly spend in prayer?
2. How much time do you *wish* you spent in prayer?
3. What do your prayers normally consist of?
4. How often did Jesus pray?
5. Describe the content of Jesus' prayers.
6. Is the Lord's Prayer (Matt. 6:9–13; Luke 11:2–4) a prayer to be prayed or a model to pattern our prayers after?
7. What does the Lord's Prayer teach us to pray for?
8. Describe a time when you honestly struggled in prayer.

TWO

■

Casting Down Temptation

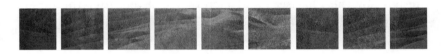

■ THE AUTHOR OF HEBREWS, writing to a persecuted people in the latter half of the first century, notes as a source of encouragement that Jesus was a sympathetic high priest, "tempted in every way, just as we are—yet was without sin" (4:15). No examination of Jesus' spirituality would be complete without consideration of his ability to cast down temptation. If the Scripture is correct, then he is the only person in history to have felt the full intensity of temptation. There is much we can learn from his discipline here. In order to do so we must, with the writer of Hebrews, accept the axiom that temptation does not equal sin.

Mention the temptation of Jesus, and most people will think of his testing and trial in the desert immediately following his baptism. There Jesus was tempted by the Devil, and though the Gospels mention nothing about prayer during this time, we would be foolish to think that he fought this battle without it. Matthew and Luke tell us that he was fasting,[1] an activity that naturally included prayer. This prayer was preparation for his coming tests, both in the desert and throughout his ministry.

This was not the only time Jesus was tempted to abandon God's will for his life.

The word translated "tempted," along with its cognates, appears frequently throughout the Gospels with a variety of meanings. Sometimes the force of "temptation" is retained. Elsewhere the context suggests a nuance of "testing," sometimes of trials sent by God.[2] Jesus once "tested" Philip about his belief in Jesus' ability to provide food for the hungry masses,[3] and Jesus was himself "tested" by the Pharisees and Herodians.[4] Even after the desert encounter, Jesus was tempted and tested, either by his adversaries or by Satan, on a number of occasions during his ministry.

If we are to uncover the background of Jesus' spirituality, we must consider Jesus' discipline of casting down temptation. This chapter will not include every single instance of the idea as it appears in the Gospels. Only those that have the most blatant connotation of overcoming the temptation to abandon the will of God and promote his own agenda will be considered. Even then there is more here than is commonly thought. Our inquiry will seek to grapple with the evidence of Jesus being "tempted in every way" and to consider how the discipline of overcoming temptation led him to be "yet without sin" and to foster the work of the Spirit in his life.

One note: we will not consider the account of the woman caught in adultery found in John 7:53–8:11. John tells us that when Jesus intervened on her behalf that he stooped to the ground and began to write in the dirt. Tradition and popular interpretation tell us that he did so to prevent himself from being lustful. This assumes that she was brought out into the streets of Jerusalem naked, a suggestion absent from John's presentation. Regardless of what Jesus was writing, he probably did not stoop to the ground to avoid looking at this woman.[5] John clearly indicates that he "straightened up" from his stooping to talk to her face-to-face after her accusers had left (8:9–10). These considerations, combined with the disputed place of this account in the text of John,[6] place it outside the scope of our inquiry. There is plenty of evidence to consider in regard to Jesus' temptations. Omitting this account does not hinder our quest.

The Temptation Account

Immediately after Jesus' baptism, he went into the Judean desert to be tempted by the Devil. Matthew and Luke note that it was the Spirit of God who led him there.[7] Mark is more emphatic, literally stating that the Spirit "drove him out" or "cast him out" into the wilderness (1:12; "sent him" [NIV]; "impelled him" [NASB]). Our experience with the Father tells us that he wants good things for us. Thus, this might suggest that placing faith and trust in him, as Jesus did at his baptism, leads exclusively to bliss and joy. But this was not the case for Jesus and therefore probably should be a cautionary note for the rest of us. The period immediately following any commitment is often marked by great temptation.

The Devil hurled three shots at Jesus. The first came after his forty-day fast.[8] Knowing that Jesus needed nourishment, the Tempter encouraged him to make bread from the stones at his feet. Physiologically, a forty-day fast is rigorous and demanding. Jesus probably had water during this time but no food. For the first forty days the body feeds on its own fat reserves, but later it begins to feed on its own internal organs. Satan's temptation here was (from his perspective) win-win: either Jesus would use his messianic powers to do Satan's bidding, thus forsaking his messiahship, or he would refuse and die from lack of nourishment. What Satan failed to realize was that (in C. S. Lewis's words), "there is a magic deeper still,"[9] the kind in which the Father rewards obedience. Jesus overcame this temptation through the recitation of Scripture: "Man does not live on bread alone, but on every word that comes from the mouth of God" (Matt. 4:4; cf. Deut. 8:3). As the children of Israel learned that manna was not their ultimate nourishment, so Jesus stood in the desert and, in the face of the temptation to "renew the manna" of his own free will (cf. John 6:30–31), articulated the force and argument of the Scriptures that food is not the goal of a man's life.

Knowing that Jesus was fond of quoting Scripture to justify his obedience, Satan attempted to engage him in an apparent contradiction of his own beliefs. If Scripture really is still in effect (the force of the formula "it is written"), then the Scripture also must be true that states that God would send his angels to care for Jesus so that he would not even stub his toe (i.e., "strike your foot against a stone"—Matt. 4:6; cf. Ps. 91:11–12). Satan took Jesus to the highest point of the temple in Jerusalem, probably overlooking the Kidron Valley, and suggested that he throw himself down and make God live up to his word. Jesus was not so easily duped, for though Satan had quoted the Scripture accurately, he had ignored its context. The psalm is concerned with Yahweh's protection of those *who love him*, not those who test him. Jesus' response was to cite more Scripture, a text totally in line with the overall tone of Psalm 91: "Do not put the Lord your God to the test" (Matt. 4:7; cf. Deut. 6:16). The temptation was about pride, about usurping God's place, as is evidenced in Satan's preface, "*If* you are the Son of God" (Matt. 4:6, emphasis added). Jesus would have none of it, for those who love God do not treat him this way.

For his final temptation in the desert, Satan offered Jesus the allegiance of the kingdoms of the world. When considering the Old Testament testimony that Yahweh rules the world and everything in it,[10] one might wonder whether the kingdoms of the world really were Satan's to give. He offered them nonetheless, if Jesus would simply bow down and worship him. Luke tells us that the essence of the kingdoms of the world lay in their "authority and splendor [glory]" and that Jesus was welcome to them if he would submit (Luke 4:5–7). The temptation here had less to do with pride and power and more to do with Jesus' knowledge of and obedience to his appointed suffering. We have already noted the expectation of the Suffering Servant to atone for the sins of Israel by bearing the cup of God's wrath.[11] In the midst of the song, the Servant is "raised and lifted up and highly exalted" (Isa. 52:13), language elsewhere used exclusively for Yahweh.[12] Glory and authority belong to the Servant (whom the New Testament affirms to be Jesus) but only in conjunction with his suffering. Glory and honor are also given to the "one like a son of man" in Daniel 7:13–14, and the connection with suffering appears there also.[13] Though the mysterious figure rides upon the clouds to the right hand of Yahweh and takes his place on one of the thrones set in heaven, he is nonetheless enthroned in the midst of the raging beasts.[14] Knowing that Jesus' role was to suffer vicariously for Israel's sins and *then* be enthroned and exalted, Satan offered Jesus the exaltation of glory and authority *without* suffering. Jesus shunned the idea, for though he would struggle with the specifics in the garden, he knew that his obedient response was to "worship the Lord . . . God, and serve him only" (Matt. 4:10; Luke 4:8; cf. Deut. 6:13).

At this point Satan left, and the angels came to minister, or attend, to Jesus. The word used here by both Matthew and Mark is used elsewhere to denote food preparation, suggesting that as the angels came they helped him break his fast and attended to his emotional and physical needs.[15] Luke 4:13 says that Satan left him "until an opportune time," suggesting that this was not the only time that he tempted Jesus. The evidence bears out that these temptations were repeated in Jesus' ministry, and knowing how to overcome them early in his ministry gave him the strength and spiritual resources necessary to cast them down whenever necessary.

An Attempt to Make Him King

Satan tempted Jesus with the allegiance of the kingdoms of
the world without suffering. The offer of "glory and authority"
over the kingdoms of the world is the offer to become king. Jesus
faced the same temptation in Galilee immediately after the feeding of the five thousand. The feeding of the five thousand and
the subsequent walking on the water are two of only a handful of
accounts shared by all four gospels.[16] Matthew and Mark indicate
that after he multiplied the food, Jesus dismissed the crowd, sent
the disciples ahead of him to the other side of the Sea of Galilee,
and retreated to the mountain alone to pray.[17] Only John tells us
the reason for his withdrawal. He was not seeking solitude simply
to be alone with his Father.

Immediately after the bread miracle, Jesus was confronted by
the crowd. Believing him to be "the Prophet" foretold by Moses
(Deut. 18:14–22), they "intended to come and make him king by
force" (John 6:15). Knowing this, Jesus dismissed the crowd, sent
the disciples ahead of him on the boat, and then retreated to the
mountain to pray. When we put the pieces together, it becomes
clear that Jesus retreated to the mountain to cast down temptation. This was the same temptation he encountered in the desert—
that of becoming king without the appointed suffering. He had
faced this in the desert before, and facing it again, he knew what
was necessary to defeat it.

Jesus and His Brothers

The temptation to throw himself down from the temple was
about *proving* himself to be the Son of God, through manipula-
tion of Scripture, in an attempt to evoke God's active response. It
wouldn't be the last time Jesus would face that particular temptation. On at least one occasion the same temptation came from
within his own family.

Catholic tradition has long held to the notion of the perpetual virginity of Mary—that Mary was a virgin both before *and after* the birth of Jesus. This idea requires a blend of scriptural gymnastics and tradition, for a number of texts hint that Mary engaged in natural relations with her husband Joseph after Jesus' birth. The account of Joseph's dream, in which he was finally convinced of Mary's innocence, concludes with the statement "he had no union with her *until* she gave birth to a son" (Matt. 1:25, emphasis added). Residents of Nazareth recognized Jesus as the son of the carpenter, the son of Mary, and "the brother of James, Joseph, Judas and Simon," and at least two sisters (Mark 6:3). Proponents of Mary's perpetual virginity believe these "brothers and sisters" to be disciples in Jesus' company. But the context is about Jesus' family ties in Nazareth, and since his disciples are elsewhere mentioned in distinction from his brothers (John 7:3), it seems best to understand that these are Jesus' biological siblings. The second-century *Proto-Gospel of James* painted a scenario in which these brothers and sisters were the offspring of Joseph's first wife, but the document's popularity outran its historical reliability.[18]

It is these brothers, these biological offspring of Mary and Joseph and siblings of Jesus, who tempted him to make a public spectacle of himself to prove that he was the Son of God.[19] As Jesus prepared to make the journey from Galilee to Jerusalem to attend the Feast of Tabernacles, his brothers encouraged him to go to Jerusalem, do miracles for everyone to see, and show himself to the world. Antagonism was inherent in their argument, for they did not believe Jesus to be the Son of God. They claimed that no one who wants to become a public figure acts secretly and that Jesus ought to demonstrate his messianic powers by doing miracles in the temple at the feast. The temptation was not unlike that of Satan taking Jesus to the temple and demanding from him proof of his messiahship. Jesus' response was, "The right time for me has not yet come" (John 7:6), ironically the same response he gave to his mother when she pressed him to perform his first public miracle.[20] The demand for signs and public demonstrations of his messiahship was something that Jesus challenged the Jewish leaders over,[21] and warned his disciples not to imitate.[22]

Peter's Confession

In the desert Satan offered Jesus the kingdoms of the world without the required suffering. Through Peter, Satan once again tempted Jesus to avoid the affliction. Jesus took his disciples to the region of Caesarea Philippi and there questioned them about his identity. Their recitation of the popular lore about Jesus (that he might be Elijah returned from heaven, John the Baptist brought back to life, or one of the prophets) was followed by a confession of their own. Peter seemed to speak for the Twelve when he said, "You are the Christ, the Son of the living God" (Matt. 16:16). Upon their confession, Jesus began to explain to them the nature of the Messiah's role to suffer on behalf of the people.[23]

Peter's rebuke of Jesus was strong: "Never, Lord! . . . This shall never happen to you!" (Matt. 16:22). Confession of Jesus as Messiah necessarily brings with it a corresponding belief that he will suffer much on behalf of God's people. Peter's inability to see this caused him to rise to Jesus' defense and vow that no suffering would come to him as long as Peter stood guard. Peter's honorable defense created a platform from which Jesus was tempted with the alleviation of suffering, just as he was in the desert. Jesus addressed Peter as "Satan," not because he believed that Peter was possessed, but in order to address the source of the comment. He recognized the temptation's origin as one he had faced before. Peter did not have in mind the things of God.[24] Luke mentions that after the desert temptation Satan watched for a more opportune time to tempt Jesus,[25] and this seems to be one such occasion. We might also reckon

Peter's defense of Jesus in the garden of Gethsemane as another such attempt to defend his master and protect him from suffering.[26]

The Garden

Just before he went to the garden of Gethsemane on the night he was betrayed, Jesus took time to pray for himself and his disciples. Knowing that great temptation was upon both him and them, he prepared himself and the disciples by praying for protection from temptation. As he prayed in the upper room, he asked for protection for his disciples from the Evil One.[27] His prayer was both for the hours immediately ahead and for the disciples' apostolic ministries after his resurrection and ascension. When they arrived in the garden, Jesus told the disciples, "Watch and pray so that you will not fall into temptation" (Matt. 26:41; Mark 14:38). Because the hour was late and their bodies desperate for sleep, Jesus suggested that they rise from their positions of sleep and "get up" and pray (or "pray standing") in order to avoid the temptation of being inattentive to Jesus' needs in this hour (Luke 22:46).

Jesus' temptation in the garden is much akin to the temptation he had faced before regarding the avoidance of suffering as the Messiah. His role as the Suffering Servant described in Isaiah 51:17–53:12 was bound with suffering on behalf of God's people, thereby bringing salvation to the nations. The temptation is clearly seen in his request for the removal of the "cup" of God's wrath. In the flow of the Servant Song, the Servant is shown a goblet of (blood-colored) wine—the wrath of God—that had made the people drunk. God promises to remove the cup of wrath from his people and never make them drink from it ever again. The horrific description of the Servant's suffering at the will of God constitutes the drinking of this same cup; and when Jesus prayed in the garden, "Take this cup from me" (Mark 14:36), he had in mind the cup of suffering ordained for the Suffering Servant.

The temptation to go by any route other than the suffering ordained for him was in full view here, and Jesus' struggle with this particular temptation was more intense than any other issue recorded in the Gospels.[28] He told his disciples plainly that he was troubled to the point of death at what lay ahead. Jesus prayed three times for the cup to pass from him. More time than we commonly assume must have passed between his request for the removal of the cup and his statement of resignation that the Father's will be done (after all, the disciples did fall asleep while Jesus was praying this). Much time, thought, prayer, struggle, and surrender took place surrounding these statements. His temptation to forego the suffering ordained for him came in full force, and Jesus, through prayer and complete surrender to God's will, defeated it for the last time.

Breeding Obedience and the Sinless Man

Jesus faced an initial period of testing in the desert in the days immediately following his baptism. We have no concrete evidence to suggest whether he was visited and tempted by Satan in person or if the temptations played themselves out in some sort of transcendental state. Whatever the case, they were legitimate temptations playing upon his mind and his obedience to the Father's will. Jesus prepared himself by fasting and defeated these temptations through the recitation of Scripture and prayer. The desert was not the only time Jesus was tempted. Jesus faced the same kinds of temptations throughout his ministry that he faced in the desert, and he defeated them in much the same manner—through prayer and proper understanding of Scripture. Jesus' defeat of temptation was ongoing and allowed the Spirit to flow freely in his life to do the things he needed to do, to be the Messiah God wanted him to be.

There is a correlation between becoming obedient to the Father's will and the presence of the Spirit's power in the believer's life. Obedience breeds spiritual power. Disobedience breeds more disobedience. When faced with temptation, every believer also encounters a decision about whether the actions and events that follow that temptation are met with greater spiritual resources or a heart that is prone to rebellion. Jesus answered the challenges that were placed before him with ultimate obedience to the Father's will and the knowledge of what real temptation and sin looked like. As he overcame each temptation, his ability to meet the next challenge was strengthened. This is not to say that Jesus was growing in his divinity but simply to acknowledge with the author of Hebrews that "he learned obedience from what he suffered and, once made perfect, he became the source of eternal salvation" (5:8-9). That he "learned obedience" cannot mean that Jesus was once disobedient and then *became* obedient (for the author had just several verses earlier made clear that he was without sin—4:15), but rather that he was learning new levels of obedience with each new challenge until his ultimate obedience (that of suffering) was complete.[29]

According to a 1999 study, an alarming number (40 percent) of professed "born-again" believers in North America have been deceived, believing that while Jesus was God's representative to lead the way to salvation, he nevertheless committed sins in his life.[30] This is at utter variance with the biblical evidence that while Jesus was the very essence of God, he nevertheless lived his life in the power of the Spirit and, as a man, effectively cast down temptation every single time he was confronted by it. If Jesus overcame temptation because he was God, then his example in dealing with temptation offers no hope for believers struggling under the Tempter's snares. But if he faced his own testing as a man through the power of the Spirit and became obedient to the Father, then his obedience becomes an example for all believers, offering hope that temptation can, in fact, be overcome. Only against the backdrop of Jesus' sinless, human obedience can Peter exhort us to "follow in His steps, who committed no sin" (1 Peter 2:21–22 NASB).

As we seek to imitate Jesus' holiness two considerations will give us encouragement and strength. First, we must approach temptation knowing that we too, like Jesus, can overcome temptation. If we continually think of Jesus in God-terms, we will miss the evidence presented to us in the Scriptures that, as a *human being*, Jesus was able to overcome the advances of the Adversary. He was "tempted in every way, just as we are—yet was without sin" (Heb. 4:15). That gives us encouragement that we too can overcome temptation. We will never be sinless as Jesus was. But we *can* overcome temptation with the help of the Spirit.

Second, the best way to prepare for temptation is to soak ourselves in Scripture. When Jesus was tempted by the Devil in the wilderness, he defeated every single temptation thrown at him by quoting Scripture. A fundamental knowledge of Scripture's *content* and *context* will help us understand who God is, what he wants from us, and what lies outside the boundaries of his will. Without a proper understanding of Scripture, it is impossible to stay within the boundaries. Reading, understanding, and committing Scripture to memory enables us to ward off sin, as David understood: "I have hidden your word in my heart that I might not sin against you" (Ps. 119:11).

This business about Scripture knowledge and memorization was important to Jesus. He didn't have time to roll out the scrolls and look for verses when the Devil attacked him. He had studied it and committed it to memory. Scripture study and memorization was an important part of Jesus' spirituality, and not just for casting down temptation. Just *how* important Scripture was for Jesus' life and spirituality is the subject to which we turn next.

For Further Reflection

1. What is the difference between temptation and sin?
2. Describe the ways Jesus was tempted in the desert.
3. Why do you think these temptations were hurled at him? Why did Satan believe these temptations would work?
4. At what other points during his life was Jesus tempted?
5. In what ways are you tempted? What are the things you struggle with the most?
6. Think about the times you were victorious in overcoming temptation. What do they have in common? How were you able to defeat temptation?
7. Think about the times you were *not* able to defeat temptation. Why was it so strong? What common threads do you see?
8. How was Jesus able to overcome the temptations hurled at him?
9. How does Jesus' example empower us to overcome temptation?

THREE

Scripture Reading
and Memorization

AS A YOUNG JEWISH BOY, Jesus was thoroughly grounded in the Old Testament, Israel's Scriptures. The Law was the platform from which Jewish education sprang, and Jesus' training in its principles and precepts began at a young age. Jesus was born to godly parents whose brief appearances in Scripture are set against the backdrop of their own familiarity with and devotion to Scripture. After being chosen to bear the Messiah, Mary sang a song of praise that had close connections with thematic content in Hannah's prayer.[1] Joseph was addressed as "son of David" (Matt. 1:20), implying his familiarity with the prophecies that point to the coming Messiah springing from David's lineage.[2] Even when Joseph sought to put Mary away quietly for her apparent indiscretion, he sought to do so in accordance with the requirements of the Law.[3]

Jesus' education took place in two venues: the home and the synagogue.[4] The liturgy in the synagogue focused on the public reading of Scripture, and Jesus' faithful attendance there would have afforded him ample opportunity to listen and learn, to hear the Scriptures

read and expounded. The home was also central as a learning platform in first-century Judaism. Parents were expected to train their
children in the commands and were to answer questions their children had about the Law and the meaning of the various festivals.[5]
This placed the burden of education squarely upon the shoulders of
the parents, particularly the fathers.[6] There may have been schools in
Jesus' day, but the evidence is inconclusive.[7] The education of Jesus,
from his childhood through his teenage years, fell ultimately to his
parents, with help from those in his synagogue community.

Luke's comment that Jesus "grew in wisdom" (2:52; cf. 2:40)
hardly seems extraordinary against the background of first-century
Jewish educational practices. Jesus grew in his understanding of
the Law as would any Jewish boy with devout parents. What is
remarkable for Luke is the *command* Jesus had of the Law at such
a young age. The year before Jesus' bar mitzvah, Joseph and Mary
took him to Jerusalem for Passover, accidentally left him behind,
and then found him amazing the teachers with his knowledge and
understanding of the Law.[8] Knowing that their child was divinely
given by Israel's God, Mary and Joseph assuredly gave him a firsthand knowledge of Israel's Scriptures.

The most fascinating aspect of Jesus' use of Scripture is the
breadth of knowledge he had of the entire Old Testament. Even
casual readers of the Gospels will note how frequently citations
from the Law and Prophets are on his lips. But what is astonish-
ing is his knowledge and memorization of the *breadth* of the Old
Testament. His quotations and allusions are not drawn from one or
two familiar passages or favorite books. He was saturated with the
Old Testament and had the ability to command, from memory, citations and allusions from its pages to justify his ministry and answer
his critics. Jesus' discipline of study and memorization of Scripture
provided the Spirit opportunities for conviction of those in Jesus'
audience, for "the word of God is living and active" (Heb. 4:12).

In this chapter we take note of Jesus' ability to read, allude to, and quote from the Old Testament. The evidence is a bit overwhelming, and our job will be no easy task. After setting forth some necessary limitations, we will turn our attention to the specific citations, allusions, and readings of Scripture in Jesus' life. His ability to call forth Scripture from memory will give us pause for reflection upon the kind of discipline necessary to foster this ability. His example will lead us finally to consider how his example should be followed by the believer.

Parameters of This Discussion

The subject of Jesus' use of the Old Testament is large, varied, and complicated. In its totality, the subject of Jesus' use of Jewish Scripture is beyond the scope of our inquiry. Our aims here are simply to gain a general picture of Jesus' familiarity with the Old Testament, perhaps drawing some conclusions about how his familiarity and intimacy with Israel's Scriptures might have been formed.

Therefore, we will not be dealing with whether or not Jesus' citation of the Old Testament demonstrates his dependence upon the Masoretic text (the official Hebrew text of the Old Testament) or the Septuagint (the Greek translation of the Hebrew Old Testament). A careful examination of the evidence suggests that Jesus' citations sometimes agree with one, sometimes with the other, and sometimes neither.[9] Jesus' use of a particular text also implies a particular theological interpretation. What does Jesus *mean* when he quotes a particular text? How are we to interpret it? Readers will no doubt be disappointed, but this too lies outside the boundaries for this chapter. The form of the recitation or allusion and its implied meaning for Jesus' ministry is not as important for our purposes as is the fact that he had an intimate familiarity with the content and overall scope of Jewish Scripture.

Neither will we concern ourselves with the Evangelists'—that is, the gospel writers'—citations of Old Testament Scripture to proof-text Jesus' messianic ministry and identity. Matthew's use, for example, of sections of Ruth and 1 Chronicles in his genealogy[10] or of Micah and Jeremiah in the birth narratives[11] tell us more about Matthew's knowledge of the Old Testament than Jesus' use of it. Our concern here is Jesus' quotation of the Old Testament, so the citations given by the Evangelists as interpretive markers for understanding Jesus' ministry will not be considered.[12]

Finally, we leave behind Jesus' postresurrection use of the Scriptures, particularly those in Luke and John. Twice after his resurrection Jesus appeared to his disciples explaining to them, "beginning with Moses and all the Prophets" the necessity of his suffering preceding his glory.[13] Just before his ascension, Jesus appeared in the upper room to the Eleven and breathed the Spirit onto them, in an apparent allusion to the Creation account.[14] But these accounts involve his divinity, his resurrected state. Our concern here is to discover Jesus' spiritual discipline of Scripture study *as a human being* in an attempt to relate what true spirituality looks like for the modern believer. Jesus' resurrected state involves pioneering work of which he is the "firstfruits" (as Paul says in 1 Cor. 15:20) of what we expect but have not yet attained.

Jesus, Literacy, and the Word of God

At the heart of Jesus' discipline in study of the Scriptures is the question of whether he could read and write. The literacy rate of ancient Israel is a complex and difficult conversation connected to Jewish education and whether or not there were schools in ancient Israel. From a cursory reading of the Old Testament, it appears that even the common people could read and write. The artisans who made the crown for the high priest were required to inscribe the words "Holy to the Lord" on it, hinting at their literacy.[15] Men were to write the commands of Yahweh on the doorframes of their houses and to write a certificate of divorce if their wives became "displeasing" to them.[16] But these examples are fraught with a host of peripheral complications.[17] The artisans who made the vestments may have learned to write *only* the words "Holy to the Lord" as a necessary function of their craft, and those who are said to have "read" in the Old Testament may have had the text *read to them* (as in the case of someone who "reads" an audio book).[18]

Jesus' spiritual discipline in Scripture study sprang from his ability to read the Scriptures. Luke's account of Jesus' inaugural sermon in Nazareth indicates that he was handed the scroll of Isaiah. He "found the place where it is written" and read the text to those gathered there (Luke 4:17–21; cf. Isa. 61:1–2). His familiarity with the text of Isaiah enabled him to go directly to the portion of Scripture that he wanted, read it, and expound on its application to his ministry. There is also the strange account of Jesus writing in the dirt in John 8:6, 8. Most scholars agree that this account is lacking from the earliest manuscripts of John's gospel. But if it did happen, Jesus may have been writing the text of Scripture that supported his legal argument against the Jewish leaders,[19] proving again his ability to both read and write Scripture.

On several occasions, Jesus challenged the Jewish leaders about their own reading of the text of Scripture. When questioned about his practice of gleaning leftover grain from the field on the Sabbath to appease his hunger, he responded, "Have you never read what David did?"[20] When challenged about his views on marriage and divorce, Jesus responded, "Haven't you read . . . that at the beginning the Creator 'made them male and female'?" He then cited the text about being united as one flesh to prove his point.[21] Again, when challenged by the chief priests and teachers of the Law about the praise he was receiving, Jesus asked them, "Have you never read?" and then pointed them to the text of

Psalm 8:2, which suggests that God has ordained praise from the common people.[22] He challenged his critics about their having read the Scripture about the "capstone"[23] and that of Moses' introduction to God at the burning bush.[24]

Jesus' challenge in each of these circumstances begs the question, Have they read these texts? In every case, Jesus asks the question in such a way as to imply a "yes" answer. The Jewish leaders *had* read these texts, were familiar with them, and should have been able to apply the point Jesus was making from their knowledge of them. That Jesus challenged them about having "read" these texts suggests that he also had read them and was familiar, not only with the texts, but also with the contexts in which they were set.

Jesus' Memorization of Scripture

If we take the Gospels at face value, we come away from them impressed with Jesus' ability, not only to read and write portions of Scripture, but also to memorize extensive portions of the Old Testament and recall them at will. His memorization of Scripture is not limited to the Isaiah scroll or the Law but involves a wide range of Old Testament texts. Citations from Exodus, Deuteronomy, the Psalms, Isaiah, Jeremiah, Zechariah, and Hosea appear on his lips in the canonical gospels. What follows here, while a bit lengthy, is a catalog of Jesus' citations from and allusions to the Old Testament. Jesus was familiar with the entire corpus and context of the passages from which he was quoting, not just with the favored passages and overall scope of Jewish Scripture. It is plainly evident that Jesus *knew* Scripture.

Quotes from Exodus

Jesus knew the Ten Commandments,[25] for on multiple occasions we find him citing them in response to a challenge from the Jewish leaders. He was able to recall from memory the command in Exodus 20:12 to "Honor your father and your mother" and the corollary in 21:17, "Anyone who curses his father or mother must be put to death" (Matt. 15:4; Mark 7:10). When tested about what kind of behavior leads to eternal life Jesus responded, "Obey the commandments" (Matt. 19:17). Challenged about which commands were important, Jesus was able to quote them at will (Matt. 19:18-19; Mark 10:19; Luke 18:20). Jesus showed familiarity with the entire corpus of Exodus, not just the Ten Commandments, for when speaking to the Jewish leaders about his identity, he quoted the text of Exodus 3:6: "I am the God of Abraham, the God of Isaac, and the God of Jacob" (Matt. 22:32; Luke 20:37-38).

Quotes from Deuteronomy

Recitation of the Mosaic Law was important when engaged in religious debate with Israel's leaders, and, along with Exodus, Jesus showed a familiarity with the text of Deuteronomy. He identified the greatest commandment by reciting the Shema (Deut. 6:4-6; Matt. 22:37-39; Mark 12:29-31), a text about God's sovereignty and our response to love him with every aspect of our being. He also appealed to the rule of the "testimony of two or three witnesses" (Deut. 19:15) on several occasions. Once he used the rule as a legal argument to prove the validity of his testimony (John 8:17), and later he employed it in establishing guidelines for confirming accusations of sin (Matt. 18:16). Jesus' familiarity with the text of Deuteronomy is also apparent in the accounts of his temptation, as he defeated every temptation from the Devil by quoting Scripture from two chapters in Deuteronomy.[26]

Quotes from Isaiah

We have already noted Jesus' identification with the Suffering Servant of Isaiah,[27] and we would expect to find quotations from the song on Jesus' lips. What we find instead is Jesus quoting from various locations in Isaiah, not just from the Song of the Suffering Servant. God's commission of Isaiah to preach so that the people would be "ever hearing but never understanding" makes its way into Jesus' explanation of the purpose of his parables (Isa. 6:9–10; Matt. 13:14–15; Mark 4:12; Luke 8:10). He believed that Isaiah prophesied the hypocrisy of the Pharisees and teachers of the Law (Isa. 29:13; Matt. 15:8–9; Mark 7:6–7). He appealed to the cosmic convulsions described in Isaiah—"the rising sun will be darkened and the moon will not give its light" (13:10) and "all the starry host will fall" (34:4)—to describe the cataclysmic and obvious nature of his second coming (Matt. 24:29; Mark 13:24–25). If anyone caused sin or offense in his disciples, that one's plight would be eternal punishment, for which Jesus quoted Isaiah 66:24: "their worm does not die, and the fire is not quenched" (Mark 9:48). And to explain the validity of his teaching without having approval from the religious authorities, he quoted Isaiah 54:13: "They will all be taught by God" (John 6:45).

Quotes from the Prophets

Jesus quoted Isaiah more than any prophet in our Old Testament canon. But he also showed familiarity with the other prophets in the Old Testament. When clearing the temple, he coupled a quote from Isaiah 56:7 with a quote from Jeremiah 7:11, saying, "My house will be called a house of prayer, but you are making it a 'den of robbers'" (Matt. 21:13; cf. Mark 11:17; Luke 19:46). He described John the Baptist as the one of whom it is written, "I will send my messenger ahead of you" (Matt. 11:10; Luke 7:27), a direct quote from Malachi 3:1. Zechariah's prophecy, "Strike the shepherd, and the sheep will be scattered" (Zech. 13:7) became a fitting description for the disciples' abandonment of Jesus during his trial (Matt. 26:31; Mark 14:27). And when mourned by the onlookers on the way to Golgotha, Jesus suggested that a worse judgment was coming to Israel, characterized by men begging the mountains to fall on them, a direct quote from Hosea 10:8 (Luke 23:30).

Quotes from the Psalms

Surprisingly, the most frequent citations (allusions are quite different and will be examined below) of Old Testament Scripture on Jesus' lips come from the Psalms. Jesus ended the parable of the tenants by asking the Jewish leaders in his presence to reflect on Psalm 118:22–23: "the stone the builders rejected has become the capstone" (Matt. 21:42; Mark 12:10–11; Luke 20:17). Later he again quoted from Psalm 118 when describing Jerusalem's plight, that soon her citizens would say, "Blessed is he who comes in the name of the LORD" (Ps. 118:26; Luke 13:35). Testing the Pharisees, Jesus played on the ambiguity of the Messiah's Davidic lineage in Psalm 110:1, which says, "The LORD says to my Lord" (Matt. 22:44; Mark 12:36; Luke 20:42–43). Psalm 82 came into play in Jesus' response to the charge of blasphemy. Psalm 82 is about the judges, those who sit in the high court of power. Yahweh addressed them as "gods" (not divine, per se, but the word *gods* is used nonetheless). Jesus quoted Psalm 82:6 as proof that Yahweh had called human beings by the divine title before (John 10:34). That Jesus was addressed as such (and often implied it of himself) stemmed from Old Testament precedent.

The Psalms became dear to Jesus as he approached his trial and suffering. Reflecting upon his betrayal, Jesus was able to recall the words of David, who was betrayed by his close friend. Jesus quoted David's reflection in Psalm 41:9 as directly applicable to his own betrayal (John 13:18). Twice from the cross Jesus cried out quotes from the Psalms. The most familiar, "My God, my God, why have you forsaken me?" (Matt. 27:46; Mark 15:34), came from Psalm 22:1, and at first glance seems to be a cry about the Father abandoning him. The second, "Father, into your hands I commit my spirit" (Luke 23:46), is lifted from Psalm 31:5 and seems to reflect Jesus' resignation unto death. But Psalms 22 and 31 reflect a larger pattern of suffering and vindication in David's psalms, suggesting that Jesus may not have felt so abandoned. The context of both psalms is Yahweh's vindication of the innocent David, who trusts in him. Jesus may have been citing the Psalms in expectation of deliverance rather than crying out in agony.[28] Whatever the case, Jesus showed a familiarity with the Psalms that is indicative of both text and context.

Allusions to the Jewish Scriptures

We have seen how frequently Jesus *quoted* the sacred Jewish Scriptures. Equally impressive is the number of texts in which Jesus *alludes* to the Old Testament. Allusions are problematic, for they are by nature imprecise.[29] Allusions are not direct quotations but images in Jesus' speech closely resembling texts shared in common with his readers. There are no doubt allusions that I have pointed out below that readers will not see and allusions that others will see that I have omitted. Still, the subject deserves attention as we study Jesus' familiarity with the Scriptures. Jesus' allusions to the Old Testament—which surpass in number his quotations of the Old Testament—spring from an understanding of Scripture held in common with his hearers.

Allusions to Genesis

Jesus often alluded to stories, events, and sayings in Genesis, revealing his familiarity with the patriarchs and the history of Israel. He appealed to the earliest part of the Genesis record when he said, "As it was in the days of Noah, so it will be at the coming of the Son of Man" (Matt. 24:37; cf. Luke 17:26). People in Noah's day (Gen. 6–8) had no idea that the flood was coming upon them, and neither will anyone know the timing of Jesus' return. He showed knowledge of the entire life of Abraham (Gen. 12:1–25:11), for when the Jewish leaders sought to kill him, his response sprung from his knowledge of this section of Genesis: "Abraham did not do such things" (John 8:40). Acknowledging his enemies' belief that Moses commanded circumcision for the Jewish people as a covenant with Yahweh, Jesus reminded them, "Actually it did not come from Moses, but from the patriarchs" (John 7:22), a fact clearly established in Genesis 17:1–14, as God sealed with circumcision the covenant with Abraham. The destruction of Sodom and Gomorrah (Gen. 19) factored into Jesus' teaching in a couple of places. He chided the cities of Galilee for refusing to believe his message and repent, saying that Korazin, Bethsaida, and Capernaum will fare worse than Sodom and Gomorrah because of their refusal to repent (Matt. 11:20–24). And his warning about the coming of the Son of Man is garnished with a simple, "Remember Lot's wife!" (Luke 17:28–32). And though strange, Jesus' statement about the "angels of God ascending and descending on the Son of Man" (John 1:51) is a direct allusion to Jacob's dream about the angels ascending and descending upon a ladder to and from the earth (Gen. 28:10–22).

Allusions to Exodus and Leviticus

Given Jesus' frequent interaction with the Jewish leaders, who claimed Moses as their champion, we expect to find Jesus alluding extensively to the ceremonial laws given in Exodus and Leviticus in defense of his ministry. Instead, we find only a handful of allusions to Exodus, and all but one of them have nothing to do with the priestly function. Luke is careful to point out that on the Mount of Transfiguration Jesus was talking with Elijah and Moses about Jesus' "departure," a translation of the Greek word *exodos* (Luke 9:30–31). As Moses once led God's people out of bondage and into freedom and service to Yahweh, so now Jesus would do the same. His conversation with Moses was no doubt informed by his reading of the Exodus account (Exod. 12–15). Immediately after the crossing of the Red Sea, Moses recounted how God provided manna and quail for his people during their wandering (Exod. 16), and Jesus was quick to point out to those who wanted the manna renewed that Moses did not give the bread from heaven (John 6:32). His use of the "I AM" formula (John 8:58; 18:5, 8) demonstrated his familiarity with Moses' commission to Pharaoh and the name by which Yahweh was to be addressed (Exod. 3:14). The only time in the gospel record that Jesus alluded to the Levitical code took place as he healed a man with leprosy. Jesus counseled him to first go and show himself to the priest and "offer the sacrifices that Moses commanded" (Mark 1:44; Luke 5:14; cf. Lev. 14:1–32).

Allusions to Numbers

Jesus only once alluded to the text of Numbers. He compared his "lifting up" from the earth in crucifixion to the time when Moses lifted up the snake in the desert. The allusion goes far beyond the serpentine post and involves the *context* of the event. For as those bitten by the snakes in judgment were destined for death until they gazed upon the bronze serpent Moses had erected (Num. 21:4–9), so also Jesus would be lifted up to rescue those under God's judgment from eternal punishment (John 3:14–18). Jesus' allusion to this event is dependent upon the context in which it occurs and is more than just a transfer of image or metaphor.

Allusions to Deuteronomy

Jesus quoted from Deuteronomy more than he alluded to it. Only two allusions to Deuteronomy appear in the Gospels. The first involves the "testimony of two or three witnesses" (Deut. 19:15), a principle Jesus employed during a legal argument with the Pharisees. Where two or three witnesses were required to make a case binding, Jesus claimed that he had no less than five witnesses ready to back his claim to messiahship (John 5:31–47).[30] Jesus did not cite the legal text of Deuteronomy 19:15, but it is difficult to imagine that as he laid out his case for legal testimony, he did not have this text in mind (cf. John 8:17–18). The second allusion involves the question brought to him about divorce in the Mosaic code. Jesus responded, "Moses permitted you to divorce your wives because your hearts were hard" (Matt. 19:8). The text of Deuteronomy 24:1–4 has nothing to say about the hardness of heart but does establish guidelines if divorce becomes necessary. Jesus' allusion to this text is clear and guides his thinking as he interacts with the Pharisees on this important question.

Allusions to 1–2 Kings

When Jesus alluded to the text of what we now call 1–2 Kings,[31] he demonstrated a thorough knowledge of it, not just a cursory familiarity. He appealed to the example of the Queen of Sheba, a non-Jew who traveled far to hear the wisdom of the Jewish king, Solomon (1 Kings 10:1–13). Jesus used her example to condemn those Jews in his presence who would not repent at the preaching of one of their own (Matt. 12:42; Luke 11:31). His inaugural sermon in Nazareth appealed to the ministries of Elijah (1 Kings 17) and Elisha (2 Kings 5) to demonstrate his own intention to take the message of the kingdom of God to the Gentiles (Luke 4:25–27). His counsel to his disciples not to "greet anyone on the road" (Luke 10:4) is reminiscent of Elisha's counsel to Gehazi, that he go quickly to the home of the Shunammite and heal her son (2 Kings 4:29). Gehazi was to run quickly because of the imminent death of the child, and Jesus' counsel to his disciples to avoid extended greetings bears striking similarity to Elisha's comment.

Allusions to Isaiah

Allusions to the Song of the Suffering Servant appear in Jesus' prayer that "the cup" would be taken from him (Matt. 26:42; Mark

14:36). "The cup" refers to the cup of God's wrath to be poured out on the Servant, who drinks it to the bottom on behalf of Israel (Isa. 51:17-23). He once asked James and John if they could "drink the cup" that he would later drink (Matt. 20:22-23). The most striking allusion comes from Isaiah 5:1-7, where Yahweh sings a song about his vineyard. The song contains four key terms—vineyard, winepress, watchtower, and wall—all of which appear in the opening line of Jesus' parable of the tenants (Matt. 21:33; Mark 12:1). As the song of the vineyard unfolds, God identifies the vineyard as the house of Israel (Isa. 5:7), and the good fruit he wanted turned quickly to bloodshed. This context forms the basis of the parable Jesus tells as the tenants of the vineyard shed the blood of every servant (including the son) sent to collect the fruit. Though not a direct quote, it is difficult *not* to see Isaiah 5:1-7 in Jesus' parable.

Allusions to Daniel

Daniel 7:13-14 and the Son of Man motif have long been seen as the background for Jesus' "Son of Man" sayings.[32] To list every use of the phrase "Son of Man" would be too lengthy here, but two clear allusions to Daniel 7 warrant mention. As he spoke with the Jewish leaders, Jesus claimed that he had been given authority to judge "because he is the Son of Man" (John 5:27), a clear allusion to the "one like a son of man" who is given "authority, glory and sovereign power" at Yahweh's right hand (Dan. 7:13-14). When questioned by the high priest about his identity, Jesus' response, "You will see the Son of Man sitting at the right hand of the Mighty One and coming on the clouds of heaven" (Matt. 26:64; Mark 14:62; cf. Luke 22:69), employed language taken straight from Daniel's vision. The "abomination that causes desolation" (Dan. 9:27) appears in Jesus' Olivet discourse as a predictive marker about the destruction of Jerusalem (Matt. 24:14-16; Mark 13:14).

Allusions to Ezekiel

The parable of the mustard seed (Matt. 13:31–32) envisions a mustard plant becoming a large tree, so large in fact "that the birds of the air come and perch in its branches." This is a clear allusion to the promise that Yahweh will plant a tree in Zion so large that "birds of every kind will nest in it; they will find shelter in the shade of its branches" (Ezek. 17:23). Ezekiel's oracle against the shepherds and the promise of one good shepherd to come (Ezek. 34:23–24) finds expression in both Jesus' statement, "I am the good shepherd" (John 10:11, 14) and in the parable of the sheep and goats (Matt. 25:31–33), in which the Son of Man separates the sheep in the same manner that Yahweh promised to "judge between one sheep and another, and between rams and goats" (Ezek. 34:17).

Allusions to the Minor Prophets

One allusion to Micah appears in Jesus' training of his disciples for kingdom preaching. Jesus warned them about the opposition they would face, reminding them that he had come to turn "father against son" and the members of a household against one another (Luke 12:53; cf. Matt. 10:35–36; Mic. 7:6). Jesus showed knowledge of the story of Jonah's swallowing and subsequent regurgitation by the great fish (Jonah 1:17–2:10) and found them fitting metaphors for the "sign" of his burial and resurrection (Matt. 12:39–41). Jesus also invoked Jonah's example as a witness against the Israelites of his own day. The men of Ninevah repented at the preaching of the Jewish prophet Jonah. How much more should those in Jesus' hearing repent at the preaching of the Jewish Messiah (Luke 11:29–30, 32; Jonah 3). Malachi 4:5–6 prophesied the return of Elijah before the "day of the LORD," and Jesus pointed to John the Baptist's ministry as a fulfillment of that prediction (Matt. 17:11–12).

Sweeping Allusions to Israel's History

In Jesus' recorded words, there are a few allusions to the breadth of Jewish history revealed in the Old Testament that cannot be narrowed down to a single text. He believed that the blood of all the martyrs, from Abel to Zechariah son of Berekiah (Matt. 23:35; Luke 11:50–51), would reach its culmination in the lifetime of his audience. This demonstrates his knowledge of a wide range of innocents who suffered for their obedience. He warned his disciples that they may suffer for his name, but, if so, they would stand in good company, "for in the same way they persecuted the prophets" (Matt. 5:12). Conversely, they were to beware of those who spoke well of them, for their ancestors treated the false prophets in that manner (Luke 6:26). Jesus wondered why the Jewish leaders who came to the garden of Gethsemane to arrest him hadn't done so when he was teaching in the temple before the people. His only retort was, "But the Scriptures must be fulfilled" (Mark 14:49), with no further clarification. For Jesus, all of Scripture was pointing in this direction. His debate about legal testimony involved statements like, "These are the Scriptures that testify about me" (John 5:39) and "Moses . . . wrote about me" (John 5:46), with no further clarification. These sweeping statements and allusions demonstrate Jesus' familiarity with more than just texts and stories. They reveal his knowledge of the overall themes of Scripture and his ability to deduce from Israel's history (revealed in the Old Testament) where Israel might be headed.

Becoming a People of the Book

It should be clear by now—from our survey of the citations, allusions, and knowledge of the overall direction of the Old Testament—that Jesus knew the Scriptures. Jesus quoted the Scriptures quite frequently; and because he wasn't able to carry scrolls around with him, he committed much of it to memory. The evidence we have extracted from the Gospels also reveals that he did not quote from just a few favorite passages but had studied and memorized large portions of many of the Old Testament books. Because he was a Jew interacting with other Jews, this knowledge of Scripture put him in a position to understand the stories that shaped Israel's national consciousness[33] and to challenge his audience (often Jewish leaders) from a common platform. His ministry was fueled by his awareness of and proper use of Scripture to speak the authoritative voice of God, even to those who had confused it with their own traditions.

Jesus' knowledge of Scripture was formed in his family context, the synagogue, and his own personal discipline of Scripture study. The Old Testament was the source and subject of learning for Jews in Jesus' day, and he learned the Scriptures as any young Jewish man would—through interaction with his parents, public readings and interpretations in the synagogue assembly, and personal study and reflection of the biblical text. The task of educating children in Scripture in our day is often delegated to the children's ministry division of the local church, to Bible school teachers and nursery workers. God's plan has always been for the precepts of the faith to be handed down from one generation to another through the family.[34] Because we are becoming more and more biblically illiterate as a nation, the work of children's ministries becomes more and more vital. But we must not neglect the responsibility of each parent to pass on to our own children the knowledge of the Scriptures. Jesus knew the Scriptures mainly because his parents lived up to their godly responsibility to train him. To be certain, his learning and astute observations impressed the Jewish leaders when he was but twelve years old.[35] But he wasn't born with this knowledge, and it's fair to assume that Jesus' understanding of the Scriptures was formed by godly parents and godly discipline.

Jesus knew the difference between the content *of* Scripture and popular tradition *about* Scripture, something that is not often clear to us. We sometimes hold beliefs about Scripture that cannot be substantiated by the text, ideas like Mary Magdalene was a prostitute and anointed Jesus for his burial,[36] there were three wise men,[37] or there was no room for Mary and Joseph in the local Bethlehem hotel on the night of Jesus' birth.[38] The only way to purge ourselves of popular traditions not supported by Scripture is to study the sacred texts for what they actually say, to know firsthand rather than believing what we've always been told. Jesus was not afraid to challenge the traditions even of the teachers of his day. And he did so from an accurate knowledge of the Scriptures.

The most impressive aspect of Jesus' discipline in the study of the Scriptures was his comprehensive knowledge of it. Jesus knew more than a few proof-texts and studied more than just a few of the most familiar books. Our sweeping survey of his Scripture quoting demonstrates that he knew a great deal of the Old Testament. He knew the context of the quotations as well as the direction in which each quote pointed for his ministry. His practice cuts against the grain of much popular preaching and teaching in the modern world, where thematic sermons and lesson plans are derived from only a few familiar verses. The public reading of Scripture as Jesus knew it in the local synagogue is becoming less prominent among the assemblies of God's people in lieu of movie clips and culturally relevant content palatable to visitors. If we are to become a people of the Book, as Jesus and his family were, we must study more than Proverbs, James, and Revelation. We must study the entire corpus of Scripture, becoming familiar with its content as well as its context. Paul called the Scriptures a "tutor," leading us to Christ,[39] and the more we study them in their totality, the more we understand, not only what Christ came to do, but also what God still intends to do in the world through us.

For Further Reflection

1. On a scale of 1 to 10, how well do you feel you know the Scriptures?
2. How much Scripture do you commit to memory? (Can you recite something right now?)
3. What are the last five books of the Bible that you've read through?
4. Why do you think Scripture was so important for Jesus?
5. How can we become "people of the Book"?
6. Describe your childhood training in the Scriptures, if any.
7. How central is Scripture in the preaching and teaching of the church you regularly attend?

■

FOUR

Corporate Worship

■ONE OF THE MAJOR COMPONENTS of Jesus' spirituality was the time he spent in corporate worship. Jesus did not seem to believe that he could worship God at home in his own way. He was a first-century Jew, and as such he worshiped according to the pattern prescribed for him and his people in the Torah. Jesus frequented the synagogue and attended the annual Jewish festal celebrations, both those recorded in the Law and at least one that arose in the intertestamental period. Jesus' practice of worship was not primarily solitary. Though at times he turned his head toward heaven and praised God, thanking him for wisdom[1] or provision of food,[2] what we find in the Gospels in connection with worship is *corporate* in the classic sense of the word, in a group setting. Personal, private worship is not the norm in the record of Jesus' life and ministry. So we examine in this chapter Jesus' practice of spending time in worship with God's people.

The *language* of worship is prominent throughout the Gospels. The most obvious word denoting worship has the sense of "bowing down" and is normally the word we translate simply as "worship."[3] As far as I can tell, it has three connotations in the Gospels. First, it can be used to describe those who come to worship Jesus in the purest sense, as in the cases of the Magi, the disciples who worshiped Jesus after seeing him walk on the water, or the blind man whose newfound understanding of Jesus' identity led him to spontaneous praise.[4] Second, the word sometimes shows up in discussions about worship, with no particular reference to Jesus at all. Many of these occur in Jesus' exchange with the Samaritan woman (John 4:20-24, where the argument is about the proper location and format for worship) and in the context of Satan's promise to give Jesus the kingdoms of the world if Jesus would worship him (Matt. 4:9-10; Luke 4:7-8).[5] The third and most basic use of the word occurs in situations where people are kneeling ("bowing down") in front of Jesus in an honorific sense. Several people—including a leper, Jairus, the mother of James and John, and the Canaanite woman—knelt before Jesus as they brought their requests to him.[6] Though the terminology of worship is prominent in the Gospels, it reveals nothing about Jesus' own pattern of worship.

Other words that we expect to show up, words like *liturgy*[7] and *service*,[8] appear in the Gospels but not in reference to Jesus. The prophetess Anna is described as one who continually served in the temple,[9] Zechariah praised God for making it possible for his people to serve him without fear,[10] and twice this connotation of "service" shows up on Jesus' lips: once as he quotes from Deuteronomy 6:13, and once as he warns his disciples about being excommunicated from the synagogue.[11] The only time the sense of "liturgy" shows up is in reference to Zechariah's appointed time of "service" (i.e., his liturgical duties in the temple; Luke 1:23). So once again, while these words appear in the Gospels, and sometimes on the lips of Jesus, they still tell us nothing about his own practice of worship.

Surprisingly this language is largely absent in regard to Jesus' practice. Most of these terms are found either in Jesus' teaching or in worship (or honor) directed *toward* him. There is little use of these terms to describe his own practice. As I think about describing Jesus' practice of corporate worship, I feel like I'm standing in a pet store, trying to catch a goldfish with my bare hands. I see it, but it's difficult to grasp. Jesus did, in fact, participate with his fellow Jews in corporate worship, so much so that the Gospel writers almost take it for granted. Judaism lived and breathed worship of Yahweh. Jesus spent his Sabbaths at the synagogue and visited Jerusalem for the annual festivals. Attendance at both of these venues provided him significant opportunities for ministry in the Spirit. Examining both of them in a bit more detail will help us understand what God expects of us when it comes to corporate worship so that we too might live as Jesus did in the Spirit of God.

Jesus and the Synagogue

There were three main venues for worship among first-century Jews: the home, the temple, and the synagogue. We already have discussed Jesus' instruction by his parents in the home, and we will turn to his appearance and worship in the temple shortly. The Gospels tell us that Jesus frequented the synagogue on the Sabbath. Luke's description of the sermon in Nazareth places Jesus in the synagogue "as was his custom" (Luke 4:16). Jesus' worship activities in Jerusalem were centered mainly in the temple. For those who lived some distance from the temple, the synagogue served as the place of worship.[12] So while Jesus was engaged in ministry outside Jerusalem, the synagogue provided the backdrop for many of his corporate worship experiences. Because Jesus spent so much time in the synagogue, we will begin our study with a brief description of the first-century synagogue service.

The Synagogue Service

The first-century synagogue service consisted mainly of Scripture reading and prayer.[13] Services were held on the Sabbath, on market days (Mondays and Thursdays),[14] and on special, holy days (feast days, the Day of Atonement, etc.). Three services were held on the Sabbath: the main service in the morning, one in the afternoon, and one during the evening. The main service in the morning consisted of the recitation of the Shema,[15] the Prayers,[16] a reading from the Pentateuch, a corresponding reading from the Prophets, and the final blessing.[17] The afternoon service consisted of prayer and the next Sabbath's reading from the Law. The evening service was a shortened form of the morning service, and consisted mainly of a recitation of the Shema and the prayers; but no reading or exposition from the Law was given at this service. The exposition of the Scriptures on the Sabbath was given primary place during the morning service, making it the most important service of those held in the synagogue.

Not much explicit evidence exists for musical elements in the first-century synagogue service. There is no singing of psalms mentioned in the liturgies. Texts and psalms from the Old Testament may have been sung or simply recited (or possibly chanted). Instrumental music was mainly reserved for the Levites in the Jerusalem temple,[18] and was banned from the synagogue after the destruction of the temple until the temple was restored.[19] The only instrument to survive into the medieval synagogue service was the shofar, the ram's horn, suggesting that instrumental music was not the focus of the synagogue service.[20] There are hints of corporate singing, though. In the generation following the temple's destruction, one of the respected rabbis, R. Akiba, remembered singing the Hallel (Pss. 113–118) and the Song of the Sea (Exod. 15) in a responsive-reading style in the temple. If the first-century synagogue was designed to mimic (or supplant) the ministry of the temple for those distant from Jerusalem, the singing of a psalm or two would have been quite natural.[21] Many of the psalms include musical notations, giving direction to the musician on the style and tempo in which the psalm was to be performed.[22]

The reason that instrumental music and singing feature so scantily in ancient descriptions of the synagogue service is that the main corpus of the service was designed for the reading and exposition of the Scriptures. All of our first-century sources, particularly Philo and Josephus, indicate that the primary purpose for the synagogue gathering was to read, study, and learn to live the precepts in the Law.[23] This was done on a daily basis in the synagogue and in the home but occurred corporately for Israel in the morning service on the Sabbath. After recitation of the Shema and the prayers came the exposition of the text, if there was in attendance one qualified to give it. This may have included direct explanations of the text or more allegorical, thematic approaches.[24]

Any qualified male could expound upon the Scriptures, whether he was a regular attender of that synagogue or not. This gave Jesus frequent opportunities to teach about the kingdom before God's people.[25] It was during the synagogue service in Nazareth—at the time of exposition—that the scroll of Isaiah was handed to him and "he began by saying" that God's kingdom was reaching its fulfillment in his preaching (Luke 4:21). That "he began" naturally infers that there were more words that followed than simply, "Today this Scripture is fulfilled in your hearing." Paul regularly found a hearing in the synagogue, as was evident in Pisidian Antioch, where, after the morning Scripture reading, he was asked if he had "a message of encouragement for the people" (Acts 13:14–15).[26] In the cases of both Jesus and Paul, the time of the morning Scripture exposition provided significant ministry opportunities for exhortation of God's people about how to responsibly flesh out His kingdom.

Jesus in the Synagogue

Jesus' regular attendance at the synagogue service provided him some unique opportunities for ministry in the Spirit. While miracles and healings aren't a part of our study of Jesus' spirituality, he certainly found frequent opportunity to perform those signs because he made a habit of attending the synagogue service on the Sabbath. Early in his ministry he went to Capernaum and entered the synagogue on the Sabbath, only to find a man there possessed of an unclean spirit.[27] On another occasion, he healed a man of a withered hand in the synagogue.[28] And on yet another occasion a woman who had been crippled for eighteen years found relief from Jesus during the synagogue service.[29] So Jesus' attendance at the weekly synagogue service provided him with some significant ministry opportunities, as well as the chance to foster the power of the Spirit in his life by connecting with the Father.

Questions naturally arose from the Jewish leadership about the lawfulness of Jesus' actions in healing on the Sabbath. According to their interpretation of the fourth commandment (prohibiting work on the Sabbath; Exod. 20:8–11), acts such as healing were not permitted on the Sabbath. There were faith healers in Israel before Jesus, and many of them performed complicated rituals for their healing powers (e.g., boiling water, mixing herbs, or reciting lengthy prayers).[30] But Jesus never mixed herbs, boiled water, or even gathered the wood necessary to build the fire to complete these acts. In fact, with the exception of the raising of Lazarus,[31] Jesus never even prayed when he healed a person. So, in his opinion, the challenge that his healings somehow violated the injunction to rest on the Sabbath wasn't valid. In every case Jesus challenged the objections of the Jewish leadership and pointed to the restoration of the person healed as the greater goal of the Sabbath commandment.[32]

Jesus, Disrespectful of the Sabbath?

If Jesus didn't obey the Jewish traditions regarding the Sabbath, does that signify that he was disrespectful of the Sabbath
or even the Law? To the Jewish leaders, some of Jesus' actions
suggested that he was disrespectful of the Sabbath prohibitions.
As recorded in John 5:1–9, on one Sabbath Jesus healed a man
who had been lame for thirty-eight years. This particular healing
occurred during one of the feasts. The Jewish leaders objected, for
when Jesus healed the lame man, he instructed him to pick up his
mat and walk, violating the injunction against "carrying a burden"
on the Sabbath.[33] Mark 1:29–34 records that on one Sabbath Jesus
spent the morning in the synagogue, as was customary, but spent
the rest of the day in Peter's home after healing his mother-in-
law. On yet another occasion, the Jewish leaders took offense that
Jesus and his disciples were reaping a harvest on the Sabbath by
plucking heads of grain from a nearby field.[34] Such actions were in
violation of the social and religious expectations of his day, painting him as disrespectful of the Sabbath in the eyes of the Jewish
leaders.

But Jesus can hardly be considered disrespectful. Several statements found on his lips in the Gospels suggest that Jesus was most
concerned about *pure worship*, not misguided tradition. When
Jesus suggested that we not bring gifts to the altar (i.e., "worship")
while harboring bitterness and anger with another believer,[35] it
demonstrated his underlying assumption that worship of Yahweh
is sacred and not to be tainted with petty jealousy. The giving of
alms was a sacred event in Jesus' eyes and not to be compromised
by putting on a show.[36] He counseled his disciples not to throw
to the dogs that which is sacred, or holy.[37] And Jesus' disruption
of the temple ministry[38] demonstrated his concern that worship
of Yahweh not be compromised by dishonesty, usury, and the sell-
ing of material goods for personal gain. Jesus can't be accused of

having a disrespectful attitude toward worship-related matters, as was thought by the Jewish leaders.

Rather, it was his *concern* for proper worship that caused him to behave the way he did on the Sabbath. If Jesus seemed disrespectful, it was only toward the tradition of the Jewish leaders, in deference to the commands laid down in the Law for the purpose of worship. Jesus healed on the Sabbath because "the Sabbath was made for man, not man for the Sabbath" (Mark 2:27).

Modern Worship and Spiritual Discipline

The portrait we find in the Gospels of Jesus' participation in corporate worship, in both the synagogue and the temple, encourages and challenges us. As there was in Jesus' day, there is in our time a designated day of worship, when God's people gather for instruction in the Scriptures and encouragement. Time and place may differ among our various faith traditions, but there still exists within our culture an understanding that Sunday morning is the designated time for worship. When we gather together for encouragement and instruction in the Word, we imitate Jesus' own habit of meeting in the synagogue on the Sabbath for worship with God's people; and we meet the expectation of the author of Hebrews, who encourages us to continue gathering together so that we may encourage one another in preparation for the Day.[39]

Jesus' experience in the synagogue also challenges the things that we often fight about in regard to worship. Modern churches tend to argue the most over the style of the music, the style of the sermon, and whether or not the service was "packaged" to be palatable to the masses. The first-century synagogue service was characterized by the reading of Scripture. If you were fortunate, someone would explain it. The emphasis upon the reading of Scripture was *the central, most important aspect* of the worship service Jesus attended. Many churches have abandoned the public reading of

Scripture in the worship service, adopting sermon patterns based on the felt needs of worshipers and topics that help the average nonchurchgoer feel good. Jesus' experience teaches us that God and his Word are most important and that, while felt needs must be addressed, they must be addressed by the counsel of God, not pop psychology and self-help gimmicks.

Simply showing up for worship is *not* an imitation of Jesus' discipline. Any competent Jewish male could have been called upon to expound the Scriptures. Does that suggest that *every* Jewish male was expected to do this? Or does it reflect only that *some* Jewish males had this ability? Whatever the case, it suggests a level of familiarity and understanding of the Scriptures absent from most churchgoing males today.

To be honest, Jesus' discipline of corporate worship challenges my own propensity for isolation. I'm an introvert by nature. I get my energy from being alone. Group events are not high on my priority list, and if given the option to spend my Sunday mornings alone with my guitar, a Bible, and a journal, I'd choose the private option every time. When I see Jesus faithfully attending the synagogue service, in spite of the hints of introversion I see in his personality,[40] I am reminded that worship is not about me. I'm reminded that gathering together with God's people corporately is good for the shadow side of my personality. It reminds me that I am a member of a redeemed *community*, not an individual with a monopoly on redemption and good worship. The challenge, to folks like me at least, is most clear in Bonhoeffer's words: "Let him who is not in community beware of being alone. Into the community you were called, the call was not meant for you alone."[41]

Jesus and the Kataphatic Experience

I served a church in the Midwest as minister of education and worship for a little over seven years. The church had two distinct worship services, with two distinctly different music styles. One was very traditional (piano and organ, very liturgical), and the other very contemporary (guitar-driven praise band). When I first arrived, both services were meeting in the main sanctuary. But as the service grew, so did the congestion in the lobby, along with the noise level during the closing prayer. So the decision was made to move the contemporary service to the multipurpose room (i.e., gymnasium). We moved the contemporary service there, thinking that the "younger" crowd would be more flexible and thus more apt to accept the change. Actually, when all was said and done, we had more people between the ages of thirty and sixty attending that service than people in any other demographic.

What surprised me most wasn't the reaction we got from moving the service. What stunned me was the number of people who were upset that the multipurpose room had no Communion table, cross, or baptistery. These were the modern "icons" in our (Protestant) service, windows that allowed the fresh air of the Spirit into our service and into our hearts. Of course, I didn't understand it. I was completely at a loss to grasp how exactly *not* having a cross on the wall, a baptistery in the corner, or a Communion table in the front lessened our spirituality.

I later discovered that I'm very *apophatic* ("apart from forms or input") in my spirituality.[42] I enjoy stripping away everything and getting down to the heart of the issue. And if given the opportunity, I'd strip away all the ceremonial elements of worship and design a service with a bare-bones spiritual experience. Folks in this category like to *meditate* on the cross during Communion rather than look at it. But other folks are *kataphatic* ("according to forms or input"). They like the prompting that visual images and props bring to their worship. They like *seeing* the cross during Communion and are prompted by different PowerPoint backgrounds to think of the various graces of God. For those folks the

absence of the Communion table in the service suggested that we
had abandoned the liturgical importance that Communion traditionally held. Jesus certainly used liturgical icons and forms as a
window to thinking about his own experience. When standing in
the temple seeing the water poured out, he pointed to himself as
the living water.[43] Amidst the ceremonial lights in the temple during the Feast of Tabernacles, he was able to say, "I am the light of
the world" (John 8:12), allowing the lights to lead people to think
about him in a particular way. Indeed, the author of Hebrews points
to many of the ceremonial aspects of the temple as having value
toward stimulating our thoughts about higher realities.[44] But Jesus
certainly wasn't afraid to challenge anyone who put more stock in
the thing itself than in the reality behind it. When discussing the
validity of oaths in the temple, he commented that it wasn't the
gold in the temple that was holy but rather the temple that sanctified the gold; likewise, the gift did not make the altar holy, but
rather the altar sanctified the gift.[45] The consecrated bread wasn't
there to lead people to think about God, but in fact was to be eaten
by those who were hungry.[46] Jesus demonstrated a willingness to
use forms in worship as conduits of spirituality, but he would not
let us confuse the forms with the greater reality they point toward.
Both styles of worship have their appropriate place. We must not
become so enamored with forms that we allow them to replace the
reality that they represent. But neither can we dismember them
altogether. Balance is the key.

Jesus and the Temple

The synagogue was not the only place Jesus practiced the discipline of corporate worship. He also regularly attended the feasts at
the temple in Jerusalem. Jesus' parents modeled for him the habit
of attending milestone events and corporate worship gatherings at
the temple. He was circumcised in the temple on the eighth day,

as was prescribed in the Law,[47] and was later officially presented in the temple for consecration.[48] Luke tells us that "every year his parents went to Jerusalem for the Feast of the Passover," making special note of the visit the year before his bar mitzvah (2:41–50).

The annual Jewish festivals were corporate gatherings of worship, remembrance, and thanksgiving. Many of our annual holidays in American culture have these themes in their origins but are losing their distinctive purpose. Thanksgiving has traditionally been a significant event in my family's history. The entire extended family—parents, grandparents, children, aunts, uncles, and cousins—gathers at the family farmhouse for a large celebration feast. This has been our tradition for as long as I can remember. But I don't ever recall talking about the Pilgrims, the Mayflower, and the provision that God gave them through their Native American hosts at any of these meals. Thanksgiving has largely been reduced to a day of eating turkey and watching football. The same might be said for any number of holidays like Memorial Day, Independence Day, and Veterans Day, all of which were designed to promote remembrance of individual sacrifices made to secure this country's freedom but have been reduced to days for barbecues. The Jewish festivals, by contrast, were designed specifically to remember and celebrate God's provision in Israel's past, and worship elements within the festival ceremonies themselves perpetuated this remembrance. Jesus' participation in these remembrance-type events suggests an avenue for reclaiming national holidays for worship purposes, a topic I will return to shortly. For now it is enough to say that Jesus participated in the Jewish national festivals and there found significant opportunities for ministry in the Spirit.

Though Jesus was brought up in Nazareth[49] and made his base of operations and home in Capernaum,[50] he made frequent trips to Jerusalem to celebrate the seasonal feasts in the temple. The Jewish calendar acknowledged several festival celebration[51] but required pilgrimage to Jerusalem for only three: the feasts of Tabernacles, Passover, and Pentecost.[52] A reading of the Gospels shows Jesus explicitly attending two of the required feasts (with the probability of attendance at the third) and teaching in the temple during a feast that was added to the calendar after the events of the Old Testament.

The Feast of Tabernacles

The Feast of Tabernacles commemorated the time when the Israelites lived in booths during the wilderness wandering. A seven-day festival of praise and offering, Tabernacles was rich with deliverance imagery, harkening Israelites back to the time when God delivered the Hebrews from bondage in Egypt and protected and provided for them during the forty years of wandering before the occupation of the Promised Land. Because it was held during the seventh month of the year, there was naturally an association with harvest of early crops and the prayer for God's provision of rain to enhance the ripening fruit.[53] The only mention in the Gospels of Jesus' visit to the temple for this feast begins in John 7. Originally Jesus' brothers challenged him to perform some public acts during the feast, prompting Jesus seemingly to refuse attendance at the feast. However, after they had gone and ceased to be a temptation to him, he went to the feast "in secret" (John 7:10). The entire corpus of John 7–10 takes place at the Feast of Tabernacles,[54] and Jesus' attendance there provided opportunity for some significant acts of ministry, including the restoration of the woman caught in adultery, the healing of the man born blind, and some extended teaching as he interacted with the Jewish leadership.[55] A full analysis of Jesus' ministry at this feast is not possible here, but allow me to offer some insight on two statements made by Jesus at the feast.

Jesus' two statements point toward his messianic status and

ministry and have direct correlation with ceremonial elements found in the temple during the Feast of Tabernacles. The Feast of Tabernacles was characterized by "light" and "water." The "lights" were manifest in the multitude of candles repetitiously lit during the feast. Standing within view of these candelabras, Jesus made the statement, "I am the light of the world" (John 8:12). This suggested that he was the ultimate reference of the lights and that if anyone were looking for "light" it was not to be found in the ceremonial temple decorations but in himself and in his teaching. The second statement was made in conjunction with the water ceremony associated with this feast. Every day the priest, in parade with other priests and temple attendants, marched to the Pool of Siloam with a pitcher. There he filled the pitcher with water, marched it back to the temple, and poured it out in the basin as the prayer for rain was offered. This prayer was offered against the backdrop of Zechariah 14, where "living water" is said to come from Jerusalem and rain is promised to those who faithfully attend the Feast of Tabernacles. It was on the last day of the feast, in view of the ceremonial gathering of the water from the Pool of Siloam, its pouring into the sacred vessels, and the subsequent prayer for rain that Jesus made the statement, "If anyone is thirsty, let him come to me and drink" (John 7:37).[56] If this "living water" really does come from God (as the context of Zechariah 14 makes clear), Jesus' statement that those at the Feast of Tabernacles looking for "water" should come to him seems incredible.

The Feast of Dedication

John also notes that shortly after the Feast of Tabernacles Jesus attended the Feast of Dedication (John 10:22). This feast is not mentioned in the Old Testament, for its origins are from the time between the Testaments. In 165 BC Judas Maccabeus challenged the authority of the Seleucid ruler Antiochus IV Epiphanes. Antiochus was a cruel and hateful man who desecrated the temple by plundering the temple for gold (found in the golden altar, lamp-stand, and the utensils), robbed the temple treasury, forbade offer-ings and sacrifices on the Sabbath, destroyed many books of the Law, put to death women who circumcised their infant males, and sacrificed pigs on the sacred altar. His desecration of the temple is called the "abomination of desolation" predicted by Daniel and referred to by Jesus as something that would take place again some-time after his own ministry.[57] Judas Maccabeus, along with his brothers Jonathan and Alexander, led a revolt against Antiochus and rid the temple and the city of him. Because the desecration of the temple was so severe, restoration had to occur before it could be used for pure and rightful worship. Once the preparations were complete, the Jews held a dedication for the temple. The Feast of Dedication (known to most of us as Hanukkah) from that point forward became an annual feast celebrated by the Jews.[58]

John 10 is the only mention of Jesus' attendance at the feast. As a first-century Jew, Jesus certainly was not obligated to travel to Jeru-salem for Dedication; but his presence there suggests, once again, a respect for Jewish corporate worship and hints at another kind of deliverance from impure temple worship to be realized only in his own teaching and ministry. There was more that occurred at the Feast of Dedication than John records (sources tell us it was patterned after the ceremonial elements of the Feast of Tabernacles). At least one significant exchange between Jesus and the Jewish leaders allowed Jesus to challenge them about his own deity and the Old Testament Scriptures that allowed for such a possibility (John 10:24–39).

The Feast of Passover

The feast the Gospel writers mention most in connection with the ministry of Jesus is that of Passover. The Passover Feast cel-ebrated God's act of freeing the Hebrews from their Egyptian cap-tors and releasing them from the cruel mastery of Pharaoh (Exod.

12:1–51).[59] Early in his ministry Jesus went to the feast and found
occasion to clear the temple of those making it into a market.[60] John
says that at this particular visit Jesus did many miracles that evoked
faith in him by the Jewish people. The next year, as Passover was
approaching (and the preceding Feast of Unleavened Bread), Jesus
found occasion to multiply the bread for the multitudes (as God
had multiplied the manna from heaven in the days immediately following the first Passover) and discoursed about what this manna,
or "bread from heaven," meant in relation to his own presence and
ministry.[61] And of course the final week of Jesus' life, ending with
his trial, torture, and crucifixion, took place in Jerusalem in conjunction with the Feast of Passover. During that final week, on the
night before he was betrayed, Jesus celebrated the Passover Feast
with his disciples. As the patriarch of the group, he had the responsibility of retelling the Passover account during the course of the
meal. There is some speculation that the Upper Room Discourse
(John 14–17) is commentary on the deliverance from oppression
that Jesus would bring in the hours to come. Again, space does not
permit me to chase down every instance of significant ministry
the Spirit wrought through Jesus because of his attendance at the
Feast of Passover. It should be enough to say that these things never
would have been possible (or as significant) had Jesus refused to
attend the feast and that the Passover background—with the slaugh-
tering of the lamb, the painting of the blood on the doorframes
of the home, and the subsequent delivery from oppression—brings
rich nuance to the work of redemption Jesus accomplished during
this feast through his crucifixion.

Modern Holidays and the Temple Experience

What does Jesus' experience in corporate festal celebrations
have to say to our modern experience? We're looking to Jesus as
a guide for our own spirituality. So how does his participation in

Israel's great feasts relate to our own experience of worship? There are "feasts" in our liturgical calendar, just as there were in the first century. We don't travel to Jerusalem to celebrate them, but the major religious celebrations (like Christmas and Easter) deserve a place in our communal worship, just as they did for Jesus.

My family's Christmas tradition holds a special place in my memory and in my spirituality. Every Christmas Eve my family gathered at my grandfather's farmhouse for a festive banquet. Children were eager to get on with the opening of presents. But there was no gift opening permitted until my grandfather had read the birth narratives (from Luke 2:1–20 and Matt. 2:1–23) from his big, black, leather-bound King James Bible. The opening of presents followed, and we all went home that night awaiting Santa's arrival for round two. Every Christmas morning my sister was awake at some insane hour, pressuring the rest of us to get up and start the process all over again. True to his own heritage, my father would not permit the opening of presents until we had read the Christmas story *again*—from his own big, black, leather-bound King James Bible. Much of the birth narratives in my memory are still couched in King James language, as a result of these annual rituals.

For the first ten years of my full-time ministry, at two separate churches, I was placed in charge of the Christmas Eve service. I must be honest and say that it was very difficult, and at times my attitude toward the service was less than ideal. I longed to attend the "feast" at my grandfather's table. To me, Christmas was to be celebrated in the context of family. But I was living and working in areas where the Christmas Eve service was an annual tradition among congregations, and spending this holy night with God's people was also a genuine expression of spiritual devotion. My family was God's people, and our seasonal celebration also was couched in spiritual things. So while my family experiences imitated Jesus' practice of attending the feasts with his family, folks attending the Christmas Eve service also were imitating Jesus' experience of worshiping at the temple during the feasts. These were high, holy days filled with reminders of God's providence and care for his people, and we were all imitating Jesus' spirituality by participating in them according to our various traditions.

The holy days and festival celebrations also have a prominent place in our liturgical calendar, just as they did for the Jews in Jesus' day. Most Christians place high importance on Christmas and Easter, while other feasts and holy days (such as Advent, Lent, and perhaps All Saints' Day) receive less attention. While these holidays have become the savior of the commercial shopping industry in America (Christmas paraphernalia is now available in advance of Thanksgiving and in some places Halloween), these significant events should not be overlooked in the worship of the church and family.

Families may take significant steps toward celebrating the feasts together and building spirituality in the family unit. Whether it's reading the birth narratives before opening Christmas presents, celebrating a family Passover meal and telling the story of God's deliverance of his people (both then and now), fasting together on Good Friday, or anonymously bestowing gifts on those who need them, there are many ways that we can claim these religious holidays for spiritual vitality instead of commercial profit.[62] Marjorie Thompson suggests that these events provide us with a "means of becoming attuned to the divine presence."[63] They are seasonal reminders that God was, and still is, actively working among his people.

Family celebrations and traditions should not push out the joy that comes with celebrating these events corporately with God's people. Good Friday services have provided some of the most meaningful experiences in my spirituality over the years. At Florida Christian College we have chapel once a week for the duration of the school year. But twice a year we host two special chapel services focused on Christmas and Good Friday. These are special events in the life of the college, and the campus community looks forward to them. Meeting with God's people in corporate, holy-day worship celebrations brings us back to the life of Christ and allows us to focus on his grace and participate in the kind of spirituality he demonstrated by worshiping with God's people. It puts us in connection with one another and with God as we stand before him as one redeemed people.

For Further Reflection

1. When did you first begin attending worship services regularly?
2. Describe the worship service you currently attend.
3. In your opinion, what is the focus of most modern worship services?
4. What, in your opinion, *should* be the focus of the modern worship service?
5. If given your preference, what would the ideal worship service look like? Do you like worship quiet or loud? Meditative or celebratory? Corporate or private? In the morning or the evening? With forms or apart from forms?
6. Think about the kinds of things Jesus did (and didn't do) on the Sabbath. As you think about the implications for modern spirituality, what grabs your attention? What implications does it have?
7. Describe some of the holiday "feast" rituals of your family.
8. In what ways are your family holiday celebrations "spiritual"?
9. Identify one thing you could do to pass on the spiritual emphasis of the major holiday feasts to your children or grandchildren.

FIVE

■

Submission

■ THOMAS À KEMPIS SPENT FIFTY–EIGHT YEARS as priest
for the Brothers of the Common Life, a Catholic monastery and
priestly community in the modern-day Netherlands. In 1429, six-
teen years after his ordination, Thomas found himself involved in
a tug-of-war between the people of Utrecht (the province where
he lived) and the pope. The authorities of the four churches at
Utrecht promoted the illiterate Rudolph of Diepholt to the office
of bishop. When Pope Martin V learned that Rudolph was illiterate, he deposed him in favor of Seuder of Culenborg. The people
had great affection for Rudolph and revolted at the pope's decision. Pope Martin issued a papal ruling that required the priests
to withhold the sacraments from the people until they became
submissive to the church. The citizens of Utrecht then demanded
that the clergy administer the sacraments or leave. Thomas led the
Brothers of the Common Life away from Utrecht. He reckoned
that submission to those in spiritual authority was, in essence,
a portrait of his submission to God[1] and more honoring to God
than rebellion (even if it was for religious purposes).

The writings of the early church father Ignatius of Antioch are peppered with references to this kind of submission. For Ignatius, the unity of the body of Christ was a central force in communicating to the world the pure and simple gospel. That unity among believers could not be achieved if the members of the body were at odds with one other. So he encouraged them to be submissive to the bishop (the elder over the congregation). Only as congregation members were submissive to the bishop would they be in submission to Christ. He wrote to the church in Ephesus, "Do ye, beloved, be careful to be subject to the bishop, and the presbyters and the deacons. For he that is subject to these is obedient to Christ, who has appointed them; but he that is disobedient to these is disobedient to Christ Jesus."[2]

Both Thomas and Ignatius took seriously the command given by the author of Hebrews: "Obey your leaders and submit to their authority. They keep watch over you as men who must give an account" (13:17). The rationale that lies behind their counsel is that everyone is in submission to a higher authority. Congregants should be submissive to their congregational leaders, knowing that their leaders are also in submission to Christ. During his time on earth, Christ Jesus demonstrated a profound submission to his Father worthy of imitation by every believer claiming allegiance to him.

Jesus' discipline in submission is an important aspect of his spirituality. Jesus demonstrated a discipline in submission to his Father that was rare among his contemporaries. He seems to have practiced submission to his parents (even when he disagreed with them), and he showed a level of respect for what is due the state that was lacking among some of his zealous contemporaries. His discipline of submission put him in the proper relationship with the Father and with others around him, enabling him to be a pure conduit through which God could bring salvation to Israel and the world.

Learning Submission and Obedience

The noncanonical gospels (books about Jesus that were deemed fanciful and erroneous by the early church) contain a few stories about Jesus' rebellious nature as a child. For example, in the introduction I mentioned the story of Jesus ending the life of one of his teachers out of annoyance and frustration.[3] On other occasions Jesus cursed to death those who destroyed pools of water he was playing in or those who bumped into him on the street.[4] According to these accounts, Jesus was a rebellious, capricious child.

But this is a far different testimony than what is found in the pages of Scripture. The biblical testimony reveals a Jesus who was obedient to his parents from a very early age. The Gospel writers find nothing worthy of mention during the first eleven years of Jesus' childhood. We can reasonably conclude that the years before this found Jesus being obedient to his parents, doing nothing that deserved mention in the pages of Scripture. We *could* also conclude that Jesus' visit to the temple at age twelve, and the ensuing panic on the part of his parents, was born from a rebellious belief that Joseph was no longer his Father. Luke says that Jesus "stayed behind" (2:43) while his parents traveled back to Galilee and that when they found him he informed them that he was doing the business of his "Father" (2:49), implying that his family relationships had begun to change. But that's not the whole story. A careful reading of the text reveals that Jesus' stay in Jerusalem was not born out of rebellion against his parents but rather from submission to and interest in the things of God. Whether or not his stay in Jerusalem was an intentional jab at his parents, Luke is clear to mention that after all of this took place they went to Nazareth and he "was obedient to them" (2:51).

Jesus no doubt learned submission from his parents, who modeled obedience at God's every request. When the angel Gabriel was sent to announce Jesus' birth to the Virgin Mary, she naturally had questions. "'How will this be,' Mary asked the angel, 'since I am a virgin?'" (Luke 1:34). Once she was told that the Holy Spirit would grow a child in her, her response was a very submissive, "I am the Lord's servant. . . . May it be to me as you have said" (v. 38). When he learned of her pregnancy, Joseph wanted to quietly dissolve his relationship with Mary, but the angel informed him that Mary had conceived from the Holy Spirit. Joseph became obedient and "did what the angel of the Lord had commanded him and took Mary home as his wife" (Matt. 1:24). Keeping Mary as his wife exposed Joseph to great public shame since she was bearing a child out of wedlock, one that she freely claimed did not belong to Joseph. Nevertheless, they were both obedient, knowing that the child in her was conceived by the Holy Spirit and would be born the Messiah. Joseph and Mary showed submission to the civil authorities as they traveled to Bethlehem for the census[5] and to their godly responsibilities by taking Jesus to the temple, first for circumcision and then for presentation after Mary's purification from childbirth.[6] When Joseph was no longer on the scene (presumably after his death) Mary showed signs of submission to Jesus, the new patriarch of his home. While attending the wedding in Cana (albeit after a bit of banter) she resigned, "Do whatever he tells you" (John 2:5). She also obeyed Jesus' desire that John care for her and that she place herself under John's care after Jesus' death.[7]

Jesus was raised by godly parents who were submissive to the will of God, even when that will caused them shame and embarrassment and required Mary to submit to her son. This kind of humble submission is contagious, and Jesus learned submission to the Father in part from their example.

Jesus and the Governing Authorities

Paul encouraged the Roman congregation to be submissive to the local governing authorities, knowing that they were established by God. Rebellion against authority constituted rebellion against God himself.[8] Jesus too demonstrated a quiet submission to the governing authorities in his day. The authorities he had to deal with were both political and religious. It would be unwise to think that politics and religion were separate in ancient Israel, for the entire society was based on religious law.[9] Any study of Jesus' submission to local authority must take into consideration his submission to temple rites as well as Roman law.

But even here Jesus' submission to the local authorities is less about his respect for those authorities themselves and more about his submission to the will of God. After healing a leper in Galilee, Jesus admonished him to go and show himself to the priest rather than tell everyone what had happened to him.[10] On the surface Jesus seemed to be submissive to the temple rituals here, but in fact he was being obedient to the requirement of Scripture, that anyone cleansed of leprosy must first present himself to the priest for ritual cleansing and reentry into Jewish society (Lev. 14:1–32). The only time we see Jesus submitting himself to the local governing authorities involved his payment of the temple tax,[11] and even there it's unclear whether this was about his submission to local authority or to God. When questioned about the temple tax, Peter affirmed to Jesus' opponents that Jesus did, in fact, pay the tax. Jesus found the whole scenario onerous, for if the kings of the earth don't make their own sons pay taxes, why should the Son pay the tax to his Father? Jesus' compliance was, in his own words, about removing offense rather than becoming submissive to local authority. He still needed a hearing with the Jewish leaders, and the offense that they would find in him was much more substantial than his refusal to pay a two-drachma levy.

We might consider Jesus' statement about giving "to Caesar what is Caesar's" evidence of his submission to the Roman authorities.[12] Rebellion against Rome was always in the air, especially around Passover (the feast that celebrated God's deliverance of his people from pagan oppression), and we could use Jesus' statement here during Passover week to represent a pacifist, submissive attitude toward the emperor. But careful examination of the text reveals that the issue was not about whether Jesus paid taxes to Caesar. The question posed to him, as a trap, involved whether it was *right* to pay taxes to Caesar.[13] Jesus' response then was less about his submission to the Roman authority in paying the tax and more about the hypocrisy of the Pharisees and Herodians, who were giving neither to God (honor) nor to Caesar (tax) what was due them both. There is no evidence that Jesus paid the tax or that his practice of it was in question. The evidence regarding his submission to local governing authority is, in every case, bound up with his submission to the will of his Father.

Jesus and the Father

Jesus addressed God as "Father" sixty-five times in the Synoptic Gospels and more than a hundred times in John.[14] His dependence upon God as the source and direction of his ministry fueled his practice of submission to the Father for whatever God wanted of him. Statements about Jesus' submission to the Father fall into two broad categories in the Gospels: submission to God as the source of his work, and submission to his preordained suffering.

Jesus and the Work of the Father

Submission language is found on Jesus' lips most often in the gospel of John. The gospel of John, more so than the Synoptics, focuses upon Jesus' relationship with God.[15] John continually portrays Jesus in dialogue with the Jewish leadership, and many times his arguments led them away from his own ministry to a consideration that the Father was really the one at work. Jesus was simply the conduit through which the Father (and the Spirit) was working.

That being the case, the Jewish leaders had to confront the possibility that they were not simply opposing Jesus but God himself.

Consider Jesus' rhetoric throughout John's gospel. After Jesus' discussion with the Samaritan woman, the disciples (who had gone to find food) returned to discover Jesus unconcerned about lunch. When they counseled him to eat something, his response was simply, "My food . . . is to do the will of him who sent me and to finish his work" (4:34). A similar statement appears in the context of Jesus' "Bread of Life" speech. When the people asked him to renew the hidden manna characteristic of the Messiah's ministry, Jesus admonished the crowd that he was the true bread from heaven and that they should begin incorporating him into their thinking (i.e., "eat the flesh of the Son of Man," 6:53–56).[16] If he was the true bread, then their incorporation of him would sustain them, as bread sustains the body. This was so because, in Jesus' words, "I live because of the Father" (6:57), and if the Father's will was Jesus' sustenance, the crowd could be sure that trust in Jesus would be the sustenance they needed for eternal life.

We also discover submission language as Jesus revealed the origin of his teaching. Jesus' consistent testimony was that his teaching—his words, his actions, even his very existence—came from the Father, not from himself. In an antagonistic exchange with the Jewish leaders Jesus asserted, "The Son can do nothing by himself; he can do only what he sees his Father doing" (5:19). He claimed, "By myself I can do nothing; I judge only as I hear" (5:30). His teaching came not from any specialized training or study but from the Father: "My teaching is not my own. It comes from him who sent me" (7:16) and "What I have heard from him I tell the world" (8:26). He told his disciples that his words were not his own but that the Father was doing his work through him (14:10). And in a bold (but true) statement, Jesus claimed that he had not said or done *anything* of his own accord but that the Father who sent him told him what to say and how to say it (12:49). Jesus' teaching and preaching of the kingdom—in every instance, in every response to every challenge— were informed and fueled by submission to the Father's will. If Jesus is correct, not once did he utter anything that *he* wanted to say, but he was completely submissive to the Father's desire in his speech.

Not only were Jesus' words those of the Father, but the work of his ministry also sprang from his submission to the Father's will. Jesus said, "I have come down from heaven not to do my will but to do the will of him who sent me" (6:38). He said that he did nothing on his own but only acted in submission to the Father's will (8:27–29). His goal was to please his Father by his submissive obedience, and the night he was betrayed we find him praying in the upper room, declaring that he had done just that. As he began his high priestly prayer, Jesus claimed, "I have brought you glory on earth by completing the work you gave me to do" (17:4).

In fact, Jesus' entire existence came from the Father. Once during the Feast of Tabernacles, he cried out in the temple, "You know me, and you know where I am from. I am not here on my own" (7:28). He compared his existence to that of a vine (a common metaphor in Israel) with God as the vinedresser, cutting off every branch in him that did not bear fruit (15:1–2). Jesus' statement may have less to do with the Father removing fruitless members of the postresurrection community than with Jesus' admission that the Father was actively pruning sterile areas of Jesus' life and ministry in order to produce more fruit in him and through him. This kind of pruning, whether in a garden or the human soul, takes discipline and serious attention to holiness and obedience. It is the stuff submission is made of, and Jesus demonstrated it throughout his life and ministry.

Submission and Suffering

We have noted in several places Jesus' role as the Suffering Servant of Isaiah 42–56. In this role Jesus also submits to the will of the Father, for several of his submission statements are found in the context of his expected suffering. Jesus described himself against the backdrop of the coming shepherd of Israel, anticipating having to give his life to defend the sheep from the savage wolves.[17] He did so willingly, in submission to the Father. "No one takes it from me," Jesus said, "but I lay it down of my own accord" (10:18). John portrays him as resolute toward this intended goal, even as the hour comes upon him. "Now my heart is troubled, and what shall I say? 'Father, save me from this hour'? No, it was for this very reason I came to this hour" (12:27). Jesus essentially is saying, "Should I pray for deliverance? No! This is why I came." His submission was most intense in the garden as he prayed on three separate occasions, "Take this cup from me."[18] He struggled with it, but ultimately submitted his heart and body in obedience to the Father's will, enabling him to say, "Not my will, but yours be done." He knew his goal was to suffer, and though he struggled with it, he was submissive to the end.

Jesus' willing submission drapes against the tapestry of the submission of the Suffering Servant. The Servant declares, "What is due me is in the LORD's hand" (Isa. 49:4). It's not immediately clear exactly what "is in the Lord's hand," about to be delivered to the Servant. But later we discover that it is nothing less than the cup of Israel's suffering.[19] The Servant bears it willingly and vows to be obedient to whatever Yahweh desires. "I have not been rebellious; I have not drawn back" (Isa. 50:5) is equivalent to the statement, "as a sheep before her shearers is silent, so he did not open his mouth" in rebellion or dissent (Isa. 53:7). He was completely submissive to the Father, and the Father rewarded his obedience.[20]

Jesus' effectiveness in ministry and his saving work of redemption through his suffering at Calvary were made possible by his willing submission to the Father's will. There were times (e.g., his agony in the garden) when he struggled to be obedient. But at every turn

Jesus testified that he spoke and acted only as the Father led him and that his ministry was a faithful response to the leading of the Father.

Submission in the Modern Context

Submission comes hard for Americans. Cultures that maintain high family structures operate by the will or direction of a patriarch, and there is little opportunity to question authority. Rebellion exists, but it is far less common than here in America, where it's almost natural to question those in power and to rebel against authority. In some cultures, it is a sign of disgrace for a child to rebel against his or her parents. In America, rebellion is fueled by historical and popular icons and is considered a normal adolescent developmental phase.

In fact, rebellion against authority is built into the very DNA of American Christianity. This country began when colonial fathers refused to submit any longer to the will of England's rule and stood their ground, rebelling against king and motherland, until the nation stood on its own two feet. There is little doubt that America, while struggling to become the land of the free, became the home of the rebellious. That rebellion trickled down into the religious atmosphere that permeated the colonial frontier. As the nation began to assert its wishes in the face of governmental authority, so also did independent preachers, ministers, and Christians assert their own independence from ecclesiastical authority. Rebellion was in the air. The colonial fathers were pushing the motherland to give a voice to the "little guy," and this atmosphere began to trickle down into the religious climate of the American frontier. Nathan Hatch, in his groundbreaking work *The Democratization of American Christianity*, demonstrates how five religious movements in early American history found their beginnings by challenging ecclesiastical authority and seeking a voice for the common person.[21]

Even my own heritage, the independent Christian Churches and Churches of Christ, owes its origins in some part to bucking against religious authority. In 1792 James O'Kelley challenged Bishop Francis Asbury over the right of appeals for circuit assignments in the Methodist Church. Asbury deserves credit for organizing the circuits in the South, but he provided little option for appeal if a preacher didn't like his circuit. O'Kelley's challenge, to "put away all other books and forms and let this [the Bible] be the only criterion,"[22] caused more than thirty ministers to withdraw from the Methodist Church and begin their own movement free from Asbury's rule.[23] Barton W. Stone asserted his independence from within the Presbyterian Church when he claimed at his ordination that he would not give the Westminster Confession doctrinal preference over the Word of God.[24] Even the mild-mannered and venerable Thomas Campbell was embroiled in dissent from the Old Light, Anti-Burgher, Seceder Presbyterian Church. His *Declaration and Address*, the manifesto for many who hold to Stone-Campbell principles, calls for ministers to practice the simple, original form of Christianity without any invention of human authority.[25] Each of these events was a landmark in the beginnings of the Restoration Movement and likely seemed to those on the receiving end as a questioning of religious authority.

The question that must be asked is whether or not it actually was rebellion, or rather a desire for restoration of the pure and simple New Testament church. O'Kelley, Stone, and Campbell all saw their dissent as God-given. O'Kelley felt that the circuit assignments dictated by Bishop Asbury were unscriptural and caused division among the preachers. Barton Stone could not agree with the Westminster Confession because his study of Scripture caused him to see doctrinal errors in the confession. And Thomas Campbell's argument with the Presbyterian Church he left in Scotland was that the church barred him from fellowship and communion with believers who belonged to any other sect of Presbyterianism. Examining such a "rebellious" history leads us to consider whether the actions of these men were born in rebellion or stemmed from a desire to strip human invention from the pure and simple faith. Is there a time when challenging authority, even religious authority, is the right thing to do? For many participants in the Restoration Movement, the answer lies in the tendency of the Restoration fathers to place their submission to God and his Word over any human structure invented, even ecclesiastical structures. In this they took their cues from Christ himself, who set his Father as his sole source of authority and submitted to him first above all others.

Submission to the Father is a tricky thing. As we follow the example of Jesus and become submissive to the Father, sometimes in opposition to ecclesiastical authority, we are confronted with counsel given by the author of Hebrews, to "obey your leaders and submit to their authority" (13:17), and Peter's encouragement to young men in the congregation to "be submissive to those who are older" (1 Peter 5:5, where the context is clearly about submission to the elders, the voices of authority in the local church). It's easy to challenge the powers that be when the options clearly involve *either* submission to God *or* submission to the powers. But what happens when the choice to resist the powers ordained by God is not so clear-cut? Submission to authority is commanded for us in the Scriptures. To buck religious authority for the sake of advancing our own cause places us in serious error.

The key to sorting it out, I think, lies in whether the submission and rebellion comes from a desire to advance our own agendas or from a sincere desire to advance the kingdom. Martin Luther, by nailing the Ninety-five Theses to the door of the church in Wittenberg, signaled his intention to question the practice of the church in his day while remaining under the authority of its leaders. That he eventually broke away from the authority of the church should be set against the great pain he took in working *within* the system to effect change. His desire was for the advancement of the kingdom and sprang from his sincere study of Scripture. So too did Thomas Campbell pen the *Declaration and Address* from a desire to effect change within the Presbyterian Church. Only much later, when their faithfulness to Scripture was outflanked by tradition, did he and his son Alexander break away from the established church. In their eyes, their retreat fueled the advance of the kingdom by restoring New Testament practices to the church. The real question for each of us is whether our bucking of authority actually *is* for the advancement of the kingdom or for our own personal causes and opinion. We must heed the caution of the example of Saul, who thought that sacrificing burnt offerings to God would be pleasing to him, when in reality he became disobedient to the express wishes of God in doing so.[26] Samuel reminded him, "To obey is better than sacrifice" (1 Sam. 15:22).

These are the situations that each of us must consider when tempted to rebel against authority, even religious authority. Jesus was in a unique position to challenge the religious leaders of his day in the name of his Father because as "Son of Man," the one seated next to the Ancient of Days, sharing the throne and its authority, he was given "authority to judge" (John 5:27; cf. Dan. 7:13–14). He alone was in a position to deliver the unique word of God for them. His *position* may have entitled him to privileges and responsibilities unattainable for us. His *word*, however, given to us through his apostles and their inspired writings, gives us pause when feeling rebellious. "Rebellion is like the sin of divination," Samuel said (1 Sam. 15:23), and many church splits that have occurred under the auspices of disagreement and kingdom advancement have been nothing more than petty jealousy run amok and a rebellious spirit draped in the garments of the kingdom. If we would be godly and imitate Jesus in his practice of submission, we too must become submissive and obedient to the Father, especially when obeying him involves being placed in submission to those he has placed in authority over us. Only then will we be set free from enslavement to both the wide and narrow roads, free to have singular vision and focus upon the kingdom, while allowing the Spirit to have free rein in our lives.

For Further Reflection

1. Define "submission."
2. Describe in your own words Jesus' discipline of submission to the Father.
3. Why do you think Jesus was so submissive to God's will?
4. Is it ever OK to be rebellious, to buck against authority? If so, when?
5. Is the church you attend characterized by a history of submission to spiritual authority or rebellion against it? Explain.
6. Think of a time when you disagreed with the leadership of your local church. Was it because you were concerned about the kingdom, or were you attempting to further a personal agenda? (This question of motive is always very difficult to sort out!)
7. In what areas are we to obey our spiritual leaders (Heb. 13:17)? Are there any areas that are up for negotiation?
8. Is it ever OK to walk *against* our church leaders? If so, for what reasons?
9. Submission can be taken too far and manipulated out of context. In what ways can submission become dangerous?
10. What do you think you can do to foster a spirit of submission in your heart (to both God and spiritual authorities)?
11. Submission can sometimes be evangelistic. Jesus was submissive to God's will for him, and by imitating him we show the world Jesus' true character. In what areas of your life would becoming more submissive make the faith more attractive to your friends, co-workers, and neighbors?

SIX

■

Simplicity

■ I FIND SIMPLICITY ONE OF THE hardest disciplines to practice. I've tried over the years to quiet my mind, limit my possessions, and reduce my schedule. But it seems like every time I try, my mind and my schedule get *more* cluttered, not less. Whenever I find that my life is too cluttered (either with material goods or complexity of scheduling), I go on an exorcism campaign, casting out from my life everything that I think is distracting me from living a simple, godly life. I get frustrated that I'm too busy, with little time to think or reflect, and I begin cutting from my life all the peripheries. For a time it works. I'm less distracted, less bothered by the things of the world, and more focused on what God wants for my life. But that's where the discipline turns back on itself. When I focus my life's energy on what God wants for me, it makes me a more effective person. And when I'm at my best, people want me to be involved.

I first noticed this in the spring of 2002. I had been working to simplify my life, knowing that I was wasting a fair amount of time in peripheral and insignificant activities. In an attempt to return to

a more simplified way of living, I created a set of guidelines to deter-
mine what things I would engage in and what activities I would
decline. I was working in a mid-sized church in the Midwest as minister of education and worship. Even with those newly constructed
guidelines in place, I still wound up enrolling in a doctoral program, teaching beginning Greek at a local Bible college, training an
intern, teaching several seminars at youth conferences, and playing
the lead role in a children's musical—all while helping to raise four
children under the age of five!

Simplicity is hard. It's hard to practice, and it's hard to define.
For some, simplicity is defined as the absence of material things.
It's been true in my life that the more stuff I have the more complicated life is. Material things either need maintenance or replacement, and in the end "moth and rust destroy" (Matt. 6:19). Richard
Foster rightly cautions us, "Time-saving devices almost never save
time."[1] Abandonment of material possessions may help for a time,
but simplicity is much more than that. In the absence of material
goods, something else tends to fill the void. Others define simplicity as quiet living. For them, the mere mention of "simplicity"
evokes images of log cabins, catching your own food, gardening,
and sitting for long periods of time whittling on the front porch.
I confess that I have occasionally longed for this lifestyle. The first
time I saw *Cast Away* I thought, "I'd *love* to be stranded there!"
But I know that simplicity is found neither in the woods nor on a
Pacific island. I hear the counsel of Thomas Kelly, reminding me
that simplicity is not about my environment:

> Our complex living, we say, is due to the complex world we live
> in, with its radios and autos, which give us more stimulation
> per square hour than used to be given per square day to our
> grandmothers. This explanation by the outward order leads
> us to turn wistfully, in some moments, to thoughts of a quiet

South Sea Island existence, or to the horse and buggy days of our great grandparents, who went, jingle bells, jingle bells, over the crisp and ringing snow to spend the day with their grandparents on the farm. Let me assure you, I have tried the life of the South Seas for a year, the long, lingering leisure of a tropic world. And I found that Americans carry into the tropics their same mad-cap, feverish life which we know on the mainland. Complexity of our program cannot be blamed upon complexity of our environment, much as we should like to think so. Nor will simplification of life follow simplification of environment. I must confess that I chafed terribly, that year in Hawaii, because in some respects the environment seemed too simple.[2]

Simplification of life has little to do with either my external environment or my schedule. Simplicity takes place first in the mind.

Simplicity is about *having a single focus.* It's not about how clear my schedule is. Henri Nouwen remarked that, while longing for a schedule in which there were no outside speaking engagements, he was disappointed when none came.[3] Simplicity is not about how little I have to do. Neither is it about how little I own. Rather, simplicity is about my life having a singular focus on the kingdom of God and orienting everything in my life in that direction. It's a pattern modeled in Jesus' life and ministry.

The Simple Son of God?

I would characterize Jesus' life as anything but simple. We romanticize the time in which he lived as an uncomplicated era free of electronic devices, complicated tax law, and overcrowded freeways. But the first century was nothing if not complicated. There was political unrest, both in Judea and in the Roman Empire. Sometimes it made its way to Galilee, where Jesus spent part of his ministry. Economic diversity revealed a great chasm between the rich and the poor, and Luke's emphasis upon the poor and outcast of society demonstrates that this was a major concern for the early church.[4] The streets were filled with talk of rebellion against Rome, and work was hard to come by for those who didn't own land. People worried about what they would eat,[5] what they would wear,[6] disease and illness (both in themselves and in loved ones), and what to do with their money and property.[7] Sound familiar? All in all, the first century was not a less complicated time in which to live.

Neither was Jesus' ministry simple. In the early days there may not have been much to worry about, except conversing with Matthew at his tax-collector's booth and spontaneously inviting the two disciples of John to spend the evening with him and have their questions answered.[8] But as his popularity began to grow, Jesus was more and more barraged with a host of requests and concerns that lay outside the purview of his ministry. Parents or loved ones brought their requests to Jesus to heal their sick family members[9] and sometimes brought the children and relatives directly to Jesus.[10] Those who were suffering sought him for relief,[11] and his many disciples even asked him to arbitrate disputes among them.[12] On one occasion his family accused him of being demon-possessed because the demands of the pressing crowds prevented him from eating.[13] At other times the crowd pressure was too great, necessitating his withdrawal for rest and prayer.[14] His schedule was occasionally dictated by special circumstances, like those of Nicodemus, who could see him only at night, and of the Samaritans, who begged him to alter his schedule and stay a few more days than he had planned (John 4:40–41).[15] A nostalgic view of Jesus' ministry as uncomplicated, free from pressure and expectations, simply isn't accurate.

Yet, Jesus' ministry reveals a profound simplicity identified in his singular focus upon God's kingdom and his mission to see it inaugurated.[16] The beginning of that new way of being God's people meant his suffering, and upon that mission he was solely focused. There was, in Jesus' life, a freedom born from a cool detachment from material goods. But this was a by-product of his single focus in life: to do the will of God, particularly in going to Jerusalem and suffering on behalf of Israel.[17] Everything else in his life took second place to doing the will of God, and he continually refused to be drawn into other affairs that distracted him from this singular focus.

The Call to Focused Living

The call to focused living appears in Jesus' teaching in a number of places. When the distractions of the world crept in, Jesus called his disciples to give their primary attention and focus to the kingdom of God rather than the concerns of the world. His life demonstrated a detachment from all that is worldly, and he called his disciples to walk in his steps.

The call is most clear in the Sermon on the Mount. Jesus warned those in his hearing against being too devoted to material possessions ("treasures on earth") and suggested, rather, "Store up for yourselves treasures in heaven" (Matt. 6:19–20). The contrast reveals a choice to be made between material things and kingdom things, between life in the "now age"[18] and life in the kingdom, as Paul put it.[19] John later described the contrast as between the things of "the world" and "the love of the Father" (1 John 2:15–17).

In the Sermon on the Mount, Jesus gave extended attention to material matters, calling his disciples to guard themselves against devotion to temporal, earthly things. The heart of this section of the sermon lies in Matthew 6:22–23: "The eye is the lamp of the body. If your eyes are good, your whole body will be full of light. But if your eyes are bad, your whole body will be full of darkness. If then the light within you is darkness, how great is that darkness!" The "good eye" was a Hebrew idiom for generosity, and the "evil eye" an idiom for one who was stingy or greedy.[20] But the word translated "good" here also has an overarching connotation of "simple" or even "single."[21] Understood this way, Jesus might very well be saying, "If your eye is single (focused?) then your whole body will be full of light." His subsequent statement that "no one can serve two masters" (6:24) again shows Jesus' desire that we give attention primarily to the things of God and not the things of the world. Focused kingdom living is the goal.

Jesus continued this thought as he challenged his disciples to turn their attention away from worry over simple necessities like food and clothing.[22] Food and clothing were much more daily concerns in the first century than in the modern age (where food is easily stored long-term). But Jesus counseled them not to worry about these things, to turn their attention instead toward the kingdom: "But seek first his kingdom and his righteousness, and all these things will be given to you as well" (Matt. 6:33). If God clothes the lilies and feeds the birds, certainly he will provide food and clothing for those who show a marked detachment from all that is worldly and focus primarily upon his kingdom.

Not long after Jesus gave this sermon, three men came to him indicating a desire to follow him and become disciples. The first indicated a desire to follow Jesus wherever he intended to go. Jesus' reply, "Foxes have holes and birds of the air have nests, but the Son of Man has no place to lay his head" (Matt. 8:20; Luke 9:58), seems harsh and strange. Jesus had just been rejected in Samaria,[23] and in honest terms he reminded this man that he was focused on his mission and would not be deterred, even if rejection followed.[24] The second man desired to first go and bury his father. Jesus instructed him, "Follow me, and let the dead bury their own dead" (Matt. 8:22; cf. Luke 9:60). Was this a harsh rebuttal? Perhaps, but Jewish responsibility for burying a family member was serious business and sometimes allowed for the alle-viation of other responsibilities. If this man really had a desire to participate in the kingdom, he needed to understand that the proc-lamation of the kingdom was more urgent than the burial of any family member.[25] The third indicated a desire to first go and say good-bye to his family. Again, what seems like a simple request was countered by another seemingly harsh rebuke: "No one who puts his hand to the plow and looks back is fit for service in the kingdom of God" (Luke 9:62). Feeling nostalgic about his family, this man wanted something more than a simple parting kiss. Jesus counseled a radical focus on the kingdom that overcomes family ties.

Only someone who is singularly focused upon the kingdom has the right perspective necessary to overcome family ties and devotion to worldly things. This is the heart of Jesus' invitation to and teaching about the kingdom. To be his disciple requires that we forsake all other things (pride, family, material goods, selfish ambition, etc.) and give sole focus to the kingdom of God.

Simplicity in Jesus' Mission

Jesus didn't just preach this kind of simplicity or expect it from his disciples. He modeled it in his own life. We have seen in the temptation account Satan's attempt to distract Jesus from his mis-sion to do the will of the Father, which included suffering. Sev-eral encounters in Jesus' ministry also show his detachment from worldly concerns and his intense focus upon doing the will of the Father, even when distractions came from his own disciples.

On a few occasions Jesus was approached by disciples with requests to arbitrate family squabbles. Each time Jesus refused to get involved. On one occasion a man asked Jesus to settle a dispute about an inheritance (Luke 12:13–14). We have no more information than that. Normally the older brother received the largest share of an inheritance, with a modest sum then given to the younger brother(s).[26] (We might only look to the parable of the prodigal son, where in response to the younger brother's request to give him his share of the estate, the father "divided his property between them" [Luke 15:12].[27]) That this man wanted his share of the estate suggests that he was a younger brother and that the older brother (executor of the estate) refused to give him his allotted share. Nobody fights like family, and knowing that there may be legitimate reasons why the older brother had refused to give over this share just yet, Jesus refused to get involved. His response, "Man, who appointed me a judge or an arbiter between you?" (Luke 12:14), is the end of the narrative. Jesus used this occasion to teach his own disciples about the dangers of greed and wealth, but he addressed the squabble no more. His response was simply a refusal to get involved. In this he demonstrated his focus on God's kingdom and spurned this worldly matter.

Jesus faced this pressure from his own family as well. Early in his Galilean ministry, Jesus was surrounded by crowds, and his focused desire to help them caused him to give his full attention to their needs, even to the neglect of his own. Mark tells us that so many people came that he and his disciples did not even have time (or make time) to eat. In response to this, Jesus' own family came to him, thinking that he was either insane or demon-possessed,[28] and intended to take custody of him.[29] They did not arrive until Jesus' conversation with the Jewish leadership (about whether or not he was possessed) had taken place. When they did, Jesus seemed ambivalent about their intentions, even to the point of offending them.[30] The crowds were so pressing that his family couldn't get to him, and when told that they were waiting outside, Jesus' response was simply, "My mother and brothers are those who hear God's word and put it into practice" (Luke 8:19–21; cf. Matt. 12:46–50; Mark 3:34–35). Pressure from his family was handled with this same detachment when his brothers attempted to force him to the Feast of Tabernacles in public display. Jesus carefully reminded them that the time of his suffering and subsequent glorification had not come.[31] Jesus would not be distracted from his kingdom focus, even by his own family.

The most memorable attempt to involve Jesus in a family squabble certainly has to be that of Martha.[32] Once while in Bethany, just east of Jerusalem, Jesus stayed in the home of Martha. Jesus traveled with an entourage, and while we aren't sure exactly how many people were there, Martha felt the need to play the host for them. In the busyness of her preparations, she expected help from her sister, Mary. Mary had joined Jesus in the next room as he taught his disciples. It was uncustomary for a woman to sit at the feet of a rabbi, so Martha expected Mary to be in the kitchen doing her part. When Mary failed to do that, Martha sought Jesus' arbitration. But he would not make Mary give up her focus on kingdom matters to help with meal preparation. His response to Martha teaches us the essence of his view on simplicity of living: "You are worried and upset about many things, but only one thing is needed" (Luke 10:41–42). Mary and Martha serve as contrasts for us in the account: one was focused on the kingdom, the other on mundane matters.[33] And while Jesus never chided Martha for her service to him, he neither rebuked Mary for choosing "what is better." His refusal to get involved indicates his own deference to the kingdom over petty family squabbles.

Toward the end of his ministry, Jesus' attention turned more and more to his impending death. He knew that his death was imminent and that he would suffer vicariously on behalf of God's people and bring atonement for sin to the entire world.[34] Even squabbles among his disciples turned his attention toward his mission, as we saw in the request of James and John (albeit through their mother) to have the places of honor in his coming kingdom. Jesus turned their attention away from the pride of having the places of honor and instead toward "the cup" appointed to him and the inadequacy of James and John to share it.[35] During the final week Jesus began spending more and more time on the Mount of Olives praying, preparing for his coming trial.[36] Luke says that from the time of his transfiguration Jesus "resolutely set out for Jerusalem" (or literally, "set his face to go to Jerusalem," 9:51). As the time drew near, his detachment from worldly things became more pronounced, even to the point of allowing Mary to empty an expensive bottle of perfume in his honor.[37] The disciples, by contrast, were concerned about the cost of the perfume. Jesus was focused on his mission, on the kingdom, and what being completely sold out to the will of God would mean for him in the coming days. Jesus knew his mission, and he would not be deterred from it by worldly concerns.

This, I submit, is the essence of simplicity: singular focus on God's kingdom. It is much more than the absence of material possessions. Jesus certainly had no abundance of material goods and "no place to lay his head" (Matt. 8:20; Luke 9:58). But there were opportunities for him to focus on worldly things, and he spurned the invitation every time and kept his attention focused on God's kingdom and his appointed mission. Simplicity is also much more than a reduction of appointments on the calendar. Jesus may have been one of the busiest public figures in the ancient world, and yet his ministry still showed signs that every activity, every event, and every conversation was pointed in the direction of the kingdom. Jesus' single focus helped make him effective and fostered the power of the Spirit in his life with pinpoint precision.

Focused Living in a Distracted World

Modern life has always seemed to me to reflect Jesus' comment to Martha: we are "worried and upset about many things." There are so many things that vie for our attention that it requires real work and discipline to shut out everything that distracts us from

kingdom living. Even more difficult is the elusive ability to maintain an appropriate balance between daily responsibilities and the
exorcism of things that have no eternal value. Certainly, there are
duties to which each of us must attend that are not overtly kingdom-
related: yard mowing, standing in line at the DMV, filling out tax
forms, cooking dinner, grocery shopping, sorting through junk
mail, cleaning the house, and doing the laundry and dishes. The
spiritual benefit of these kinds of activities is difficult to see. (I
reminded my wife once, as she was frustrated about how much
laundry there was to do when our children were all under seven,
that laundry was "spiritual activity"—it was the first thing Jesus did
in his resurrected state [John 20:7].) Some things simply must be
attended to, and though they don't seem to be overtly spiritual or
focused on God and his kingdom, they must be done or life for us
would become quite difficult.

I mention all of this because, as you're reading my comments
about Jesus' refusal to engage in anything that wasn't overtly kingdom related, you may be hearing a call to abandon every single
thing that has no overt benefit to the kingdom and elope to a
quiet place to spend the rest of your days in prayer and medita-
tion. The desert monks certainly considered this a valid response
to the corruption and complication of the world.[38] But this was
not Jesus' response to the pressing crowds, nor should it be ours.
Reflecting the wisdom of a later time François Fénelon cautioned
those under his care that the refusal to attend to daily responsibilities in order to become more spiritual was a dangerous and decep-
tive philosophy. "People who neglect their duties to 'spend more
time with God' deceive themselves. You won't get closer to God by
being irresponsible and calling it 'spiritual.'"[39]

So how exactly is a person supposed to practice simplicity?
How does a person have "singular focus" in the midst of everyday life, where chores and job responsibilities may have no explicit

kingdom value? If we're defining it as being completely sold out to and focused on God's kingdom, then the things we do must become focused. In short, it's a matter of perspective. Jesus had his life in order, and it had little to do with how many material possessions he had or how many appointments appeared on his calendar. His life was focused, "simple" in the sense that he knew what his mission was and let nothing stand in the way of accomplishing it. Our mission will never be quite the same as his (to suffer for the redemption of God's people) but each of us has a responsibility to simplify life in view of God's kingdom. When kingdom living becomes the focus of life, all other pressures and responsibilities take second place. Every action, every deed, every hour of work and play becomes a kingdom matter. I not only begin thinking, "How does this serve the reign of God in my life and in the world?" but I also begin to think, "How can I *perform* this task in a kingdomly manner?" What am I here to do, and how do my possessions and appointments serve God's purpose for my life? Only when that primary kingdom focus is in view do other pressures and responsibilities seem trite in comparison, giving me the perspective necessary to remove that distraction from my life in favor of something more substantial, more real, and more eternal.

I spent a little over seven years ministering in the greater Detroit area. While located there I was once called by the St. Jude Children's Research Hospital to do some fund-raising. A friend had given them my name, prompting them to ask if they could put me in a jail cell, with nothing but a phone, until I raised a thousand dollars for their research. I politely declined. I'm not a salesman. I'm no good at it. So I told them, politely, that I was in favor of their efforts to raise more money for medical research but that participating with them was not part of what I was called to do. That activity, humanitarian in its own right, would have distracted me from my kingdom purpose and put me on another path, one that would have taken focus away from my appointed ministry and mission. Perhaps that sounds harsh, but it is no less harsh than Jesus' counsel to forsake all worldly things, even family ties, to devote full attention to him.[40]

Before I conclude I probably should say a word about simplicity in the area of material possessions. It's easy to make a case for simplicity in material possessions from the life of Jesus because he didn't have any—at least not to the extent that he had a home, or land, or boats, and so on. While Jesus was known to have called folks to give up everything they owned,[41] this call seemed to be directed specifically at the one for whom material possessions stood in the way of full participation in the kingdom. It was not a universal call to poverty. And yet, I find that so many in the Western world are bound by their possessions. We purchase, own, and throw away more stuff in a year's time than many people across the world ever will in a lifetime. Simplicity in material goods is needed, and I tend to agree with Richard Foster's assessment that "the majority of Christians have never seriously wrestled with the problem of simplicity."[42] And of those who attempt it, many find it difficult to maintain that simplicity long-term. For those of you reading this who are drawn to the idea and are looking for serious counsel, let me suggest Foster's *Freedom of Simplicity* as a launching point.

Imitating Jesus in the area of simplicity requires that we cast off all distractions and become "simple," "single," and "focused." Anything less and we allow the distractions of the world to fight for our attention. A man cannot "serve two masters" (Matt. 6:24). If he does, he will be a "double-minded man, unstable in all he does" (James 1:8).

For Further Reflection

1. Would you characterize your life as simple or complicated?
2. What are some activities you wouldn't mind cutting out of your schedule?
3. If you did this, what activities would you like to focus more of your attention on?
4. Do you think you own too many possessions? If so, what material goods do you purchase in excess?
5. How did Jesus practice simplicity?
6. Do the activities and events at your local church promote simple, kingdom-minded living, or do they promote busyness and dependence?
7. In what ways can you promote kingdom focus in your home, in your church, and in your personal schedule?

■

SEVEN

Care for the Oppressed

■ WHEN I FIRST MET RUSS HARRINGTON, he was superintendent of St. Allen's High School.[1] It was 1996, and I was working as a youth minister in a small town in West Virginia. I had
received an invitation from him to come and serve on the Sensitive
Issues Task Force, a collection of individuals and community leaders helping to integrate African Americans, Latinos, Asians, gays,
and lesbians into a school system that was 96 percent white and
Protestant. Students with these minority backgrounds were often
the victims of hate crimes there, and Russ Harrington was trying to
get a handle on it. I knew I would have a problem with the lifestyles
section of this project (you've probably picked up by now that I'm a
pretty conservative Christian), but I was excited about the integra-
tion of the ethnic groups and saw this as an opportunity to gain a
hearing within the public school system. Moreover, it was a chance
to do something of kingdom significance outside the four walls of
my church office.

It wasn't long until I learned that Russ Harrington was a
Christian and had at one time been a fundamentalist Baptist

preacher. I was perplexed, even shocked, to learn that a Jerry Falwell-type preacher would be leading the charge in the public school system for tolerance of gays and lesbians—until I heard his story. Russ Harrington's ministry had always been for the outcast.

Before coming to the St. Allen's school system, Russ Harrington had preached at a small church in a very small West Virginia town. Russ ate lunch once a week at the local tavern (they had the best sandwiches in town) and became known by the regular customers. Of course, this was a tavern. It was the place men went to drink. He spent enough time there that the men befriended him and knew him by name.

Russ sensed a connection with the men and wanted to pursue this opportunity. He asked the owner of the tavern if he could leave extra Sunday bulletins around the tables on Monday morning. They were extras and destined to be thrown away. The owner reluctantly agreed. The men in the tavern quickly noticed that Russ's name appeared on the back of the bulletin. So they asked their new friend if he would explain some of the things in the sermon outline. That turned into a request to preach his sermons in the tavern on Mondays over lunch, and before anyone knew it, these guys were having church in the town bar.

Knowing that their spiritual vitality and conversion meant that they would have to face the town and publicly repent, Russ began encouraging these men to attend the Sunday worship services. They didn't at first. Church was the last place these guys would be expected to appear in a small town, and if they did, they would surely be the week's topic of gossip. But eventually a few did, and then a few more, until the day when too many of them showed up together. On that day the board of deacons immediately called an emergency meeting and ordered Russ Harrington to either tell these men to leave or find another job.

Again, when I first met Russ Harrington, he was the superintendent of St. Allen's High School.

Russ Harrington never consciously stated it to me. He may not have even known it at the time. But he knew and practiced a component of spirituality that was vibrant in the life of Jesus. Jesus regularly welcomed outsiders. Whether they were disenfranchised by society in general or ostracized by the religious community in particular, Jesus regularly welcomed all who came to him and treated them with great dignity and respect. Judging by Russ Harrington's experience, it's a lot easier to talk about than to do.

Jesus and the Outcasts

Jesus regularly practiced the discipline of welcoming into his company those who were not part of the mainstream. Of course, there were those *within* the mainstream whom he accepted and spent time with, like Pharisees, teachers of the Law, scribes, rulers, centurions, synagogue attendants, and fishermen. But while most of us are prone to spend our time within our own groups ("tribes" as the kids call them these days), Jesus seems to have intentionally made as part of his "tribe" those who otherwise would have been excluded.

What I am describing is the discipline of hospitality, which has received little attention in the discussion of spiritual gifts and disciplines. Therefore, we will have to chart our course carefully, noting exactly *the people* Jesus spent time with and what challenge he offered to the religious establishment (both then and now) by doing so. Jesus primarily opened his influence to four disenfranchised groups of his day: tax collectors, "sinners," Gentiles, and the poor.

Tax Collectors

Tax collectors were a hated group of people in the first century. To say that they were the equivalent of the modern IRS agent is a misnomer and misses the sense of treason that often accompanied the trade. Rome demanded taxes from the countries it occupied. Rome offered certain amenities to countries under its rule—roads, aqueducts, peace secured by military rule—and those amenities had to be paid for. It would have made little sense to send Roman soldiers door to door to collect taxes from the Jewish people. To ease the burden, Rome hired tax collectors from the native country (in this case Jews) to collect those taxes from among their own people. Because they worked for the occupying enemy, these Jewish tax collectors were considered traitors by their countrymen. Tax collectors often advanced the money to their employers, suggesting that they were people of considerable wealth. They made their living by usury and were commonly associated with robbers and brothel-keepers.[2] Tax collectors were generally regarded to have forfeited their citizenship in Israel, thereby ostracizing them from God and his people in the eyes of the religious establishment.[3]

Though most Jews in his day avoided tax collectors, Jesus made it his practice to welcome them into his hearing. One of his disciples, Matthew, was a tax collector; and when Matthew accepted the call to discipleship, many other tax collectors were moved to check out Jesus over dinner in Matthew's home, so many, in fact, that it prompted the Pharisees to question Jesus' disciples about it.[4]

Zacchaeus was known as a "chief tax collector," a term denoting either some standing among tax collectors, or one who employed a number of tax collectors under his jurisdiction. Luke 19:1-10 tells us that Jesus advanced himself to Zacchaeus's home for dinner, and, as a result of his encounter with Jesus, Zacchaeus committed to repay anyone he had cheated up to four times the amount. This repentance was impressive to Jesus, so much that he declared Zacchaeus a "son of Abraham."

Repentance was a natural by-product of and a catalyst for the presence of the tax collectors and "sinners" in Jesus' hearing. Jesus' fellowship with them (particularly over meals) caused great consternation among the Jewish leadership.[5] But Jesus' response was always pointed toward their repentance. Because of their repentance, "the tax collectors and the prostitutes [were] entering the kingdom of God" ahead of the Jewish leaders (Matt. 21:31). The parables of the lost sheep, coin, and son in Luke 15 all arose from a dispute about Jesus' table fellowship with tax collectors and sinners. Each parable seems to end with an overabundance of joy over one sinner repenting. Jesus was gracious toward them, and his grace resulted in their repentance, suggesting that Jesus not only welcomed them as friends but also preached the gospel of the kingdom to them once he did so.

"Sinners"

The term *tax collector* is often coupled with the word *sinner* in the Gospels. The term *sinner* carried a wide range of meaning in first-century Judaism. Traditionally the term was applied to those who disagreed with the Pharisaic interpretation of the Law. Since the Pharisees enforced the will of God in the eyes of the populace, anyone who disagreed with their tradition might be labeled a "sinner."[6] Recent studies have shown that the term denoted an aggressively immoral lifestyle, a life that was opposed to God and his Law. It applied not just to the Gentiles outside the Law but also to those within Israel who knew the Law and had forsaken it.[7] In a couple of places the context of Luke suggests that we may be dealing with some who were involved in sexually promiscuous lifestyles, even prostitutes. In the parables of Luke 15, Luke seems to identify the "sinners" (v. 1), with the "prostitutes" with whom the younger brother had squandered his inheritance (v. 30). Earlier, Luke had identified the woman who anointed Jesus in Galilee as one "who had lived a sinful life" (7:37). That the Pharisee objected to the woman's actions because of "what kind of woman she is" (v. 39) suggests that there was something overtly sensuous about this

scene, pointing again to a meaning closely related to sexual promiscuity. Whether "sinners" were those who disagreed with the
Pharisees or those who represented the most rebellious attitudes
toward God in ancient Israel, they were definitely ostracized by
the religious establishment in Israel.

The most notable "sinner" in the Gospel record is arguably
this woman who anointed Jesus in Galilee. She is unnamed (and
not Mary Magdalene) and described by Luke only as "a woman
who had lived a sinful life in that town" (7:37; lit., "a certain
woman who was a 'sinner' in the city"). She anointed Jesus with
perfume and began to caress his feet with her tears and her hair.
The whole scenario looked inappropriate to Simon, the Pharisee.
But Jesus' rebuttal was simply that she had been forgiven much,
and this anointing was a manifestation of her repentance. Again,
we find Jesus describing his welcome of these outcasts in terms of
their repentance. Their repentance may not have been the condition for Jesus' acceptance of them, but it certainly seems clear in
his responses to the accusations of the Jewish leaders that it was
the condition of his *continuing* to welcome them in and even a by-
product of his hospitality and teaching.

Gentiles

Ancient Jews divided the world into two groups: Jews and
Gentiles. Godly people in every age have struggled with the exact
relationship between faith and culture, whether to adapt the faith
to culture or forsake culture altogether. Jews of Jesus' day were no
different. Scot McKnight has identified several tendencies of Jews
in Jesus' day that helped make the Jewish faith palatable to Gentiles and several foundational beliefs that alienated them.[8] Jesus
sometimes said things like "Do not even pagans do that?" (Matt.
5:47) and "Treat him as you would a pagan" (Matt. 18:17). At first
glance it seems that Jesus was referring to the Gentiles, or pagans,

negatively. But his audience in those situations were Jews, and he was using the word *pagan* in the sense of "outsider" in both discussions.[9] By and large, Jesus had no problem allowing Gentiles to participate in the kingdom. He welcomed them on the same basis that he welcomed tax collectors and sinners: on the basis of their faith in him and their demonstrated repentance. He did not seem to make the faith more palatable to them but offered them acceptance into his presence as a way of gaining a hearing among them.

Jesus' practice of including Gentiles in his kingdom work puts feet to many promises made in the Old Testament. God's plan, since the time of Abraham, had been to make him "a father of *many* nations" (Gen. 17:4–5, emphasis added), and the Lord declared that his Servant would be "a light for the Gentiles," bringing salvation to them (Isa. 49:6). Isaiah's vision of the great messianic banquet envisions a feast for "all peoples . . . all nations" (Isa. 25:6–9, where the "all peoples" then become "his people") in the same way that Joel's vision encompasses God's Spirit poured out on "all people" (Joel 2:28). This theme of the welcoming of the Gentiles begins to grow in the Gospel accounts of Jesus' ministry, as the pagans from the East came to worship him (Matt. 2:1–12), and as Jesus talked about "sheep that are not of this sheep pen" (John 10:16) and of many who would "come from the east and the west, and . . . take their places at the feast" (Matt. 8:11). It culminated in the upper room, as Jesus declared that his body and blood would be shed "for many" (Matt. 26:28; Mark 14:24). These themes then came to fruition in Acts 10, as Peter's vision led to the conversion of the Roman centurion Cornelius and a vigorous debate among the apostles about the nature of Gentile faith (Acts 15). The rest of the book of Acts recounts the spread of the gospel to the Gentiles in the evangelistic ministry of Paul.

Jesus' interaction with the centurion is representative of the way he welcomed interested outsiders (non-Jews) into his presence.

The centurion came to Jesus with a request to heal his ailing servant.[10] Jesus promised to go at once to heal him, but the centurion offered a proposal that Jesus simply give the word, knowing that as Jesus uttered it his servant would be healed. Perhaps he believed that Jesus had the *power* to give orders and have them obeyed, just as the soldiers under his command obeyed his orders. More likely, he believed that, just as he was a conduit through which the emperor directed the Roman army, so Jesus was a conduit through whom the higher power of God Almighty flowed. Either way, Jesus praised him as having more faith than any he'd met in Israel.

Jesus was not shy about including Gentiles (like the centurion), Samaritans,[11] and a woman from Syro-Phoenicia.[12] Often these folks had more faith in him and demonstrated more willingness to participate in his kingdom vision than some of his own people. Jesus foresaw the time when, because of the rejection of the Jews, the kingdom of God would be taken away from them "and given to a people who will produce its fruit" (Matt. 21:43). It's not that he *favored* Gentiles and "outsiders" over his own people. Rather, he made a habit of opening his arms to those who would be willing participants in the work that God was doing through him, be they Jew or Gentile. And in many cases the Gentiles had more faith in him than his own people.

The Poor

Jesus was surrounded by multitudes. We have already noted that he was so pressed by the crowds that he often had to withdraw and seek solitude. The crowds were by no means homogeneous but certainly were comprised mostly of what scholars call "the people of the land." These were the common, everyday people, and most studies suggest that they were comprised of the poor.[13] Jesus had rich people in his company. If Matthew advanced Rome the money for his annual levy, then he certainly was a person of some affluence. John was known to the high priest,[14] suggesting that he was a person of some influence or importance. Pharisees, scribes, centurions, Herodians, and rich young rulers were among the socially prominent folks associated with Jesus in the Gospels. But the crowds about him consisted mostly of the poor.

It would have been easy for Jesus to hang out exclusively with the "important" people. In fact, one could argue that his ministry would have gained a more influential hearing had he strategically influenced the more socially elite among his disciples and rejected the "insignificants." But he didn't do that. His statement in the Sermon on the Plain, "Blessed are you who are poor" (Luke 6:20), showed his compassion for them, while its antithesis, "Woe to you who are rich" (Luke 6:24), demonstrated Jesus' view that wealth is one of the foremost obstacles to participation in the kingdom.[15]

Jesus' welcome of the poor reflects one of the focal points of God's compassion. Sometimes they needed healing, like the woman with the issue of blood who had spent her money on doctors to no avail, the lepers, or the blind beggars.[16] At other times they needed food, and Jesus provided it when he fed the five thousand and later the four thousand.[17] But his ministry with them was never just about the material provision or the healing. He was anointed specifically "to preach good news to the poor" (Luke 4:18), and he once pointed the disciples of John the Baptist to the evangelization of the poor as proof that he was in fact the promised Messiah.[18] Jesus cared for them, both materially and spiritually.

Jesus also taught that care for the poor is an integral part of one's relationship with God. He challenged the rich young ruler to sell all he had and give to the poor (a request that was not honored),[19] and he challenged the Jewish leaders to give to the poor and invite them to their expensive banquets.[20] Zacchaeus was so moved by Jesus' teaching that he immediately vowed to give half his possessions to the poor (Luke 19:8). Jesus was a friend of the poor. He continually welcomed them into his presence and challenged others to do the same.

Ironically, one statement made in the Gospels that points toward Jesus' practice of helping the poor comes from Judas. During the final week Mary, the sister of Martha and Lazarus, took an expensive jar of perfume and poured the contents over Jesus' feet and head.[21] Judas objected that the perfume (which cost about a year's wages) could have been sold and the money given to the poor (John 12:4–5). Of course, Judas didn't care about the poor, and John plainly says so (v. 6). So why did he say this? He didn't actually want to help the poor, but he believed that saying this would resonate with Jesus enough to evoke a chastisement of Mary for being wasteful. This suggests that Jesus was regularly in the habit of helping the poor financially. If not, Judas wouldn't have expected his objection to gain a hearing. When Judas left to betray Jesus, the disciples naturally assumed that Jesus had told him to go and give money to the poor (John 13:29), giving further indication that Jesus' practice and teaching on the matter was well known to his disciples.

God's concern for the poor, the alien, the orphan, and the widow (those disenfranchised from society) is well attested in the Old Testament literature. David said, "The LORD is close to the brokenhearted" (Ps. 34:18) and declared that the Lord rescues "the poor from those too strong for them" (Ps. 35:10). Josiah is described as one who defended the cause of the poor and needy and, in turn, knew the Lord (Jer. 22:16). In several texts about the coming Good Shepherd, God chastised the shepherds of Israel for not binding up the injured, caring for the weak, and protecting the flock (Jer. 23:1–2; Ezek. 34:1–6). It was appointed for Messiah to "give decisions for the poor of the earth" (Isa. 11:4), "preach good news to the poor," and "bind up the brokenhearted" (Isa. 61:1). God has always been concerned with the plight of the poor.

Pure and right spirituality in his eyes is demonstrated when God's people care for the poor and needy (James 1:27).

Welcoming the Outcasts

Jesus continually surrounded himself with all the wrong people. Gentiles, tax collectors, "sinners," and "the people of the land" are just a few of the groups we have mentioned. We also could have mentioned lepers, the blind, the mute, demoniacs, those caught in adultery, invalids, Samaritans, widows, and children. Each of these groups were either ostracized or deemed insignificant by all the people that seemed to matter in the ancient world. Jesus rejected this kind of thinking. In God's view, these ostracized people needed *more* care because of their circumstances. Jesus gave it to them willingly.

Of course, Jesus didn't just go *looking* for poor, disenfranchised people to hang out with. He didn't come to include the outcasts and exclude the "in crowd," and he didn't come to help the poor at the expense of the rich. It was simply part of his character and discipline to spend time with those who needed a voice. I think this gracious demeanor was formed in him by his own study of Scripture, which led him to a knowledge of God's intense longing for the outcast. Part of his spiritual discipline was to enact what he knew the Father had decreed for Israel in her Scriptures. But Jesus did not make the mistake of ostracizing the rich and wealthy in favor of the poor. He had the rich and wealthy among his followers and gave them a hearing whenever they wanted it, for, as Howard Thurman put it, "The ethical demand upon the more privileged and the underprivileged is the same."[22] But his conscience was sensitive to the outcasts, and he made sure that they were included and welcomed.

Christian spirituality is about becoming godly. It's about demonstrating the kinds of godly qualities and characteristics we see manifested in the life of Jesus. If we would be godly, we must think and act like God thinks and acts, and Jesus' example demonstrates for us that God deeply cares about the outsiders. It has always been his plan to welcome the outsiders into his kingdom.

Who are the outsiders today? Who are the modern-day Gentiles who are continually spurned by the religious community? Who are the "sinners" and traitors to God's people? Russ Harrington would tell you they are alcoholics and drug addicts. They're ex-convicts and sex addicts. They're drinkers, smokers, single parents, illegitimate children, atheists, Muslims, Buddhists, Hindus, and, yes, homosexuals. In the course of my life, I have known several churches filled with people for whom the above-mentioned groups were seldom welcome. There were always godly people who knew better and tried to hold out the faith for everyone. And to be sure, there was talk of "whosoever will may come." But by and large, the overwhelming voice rang out, "If you're not like us, you're not welcome here." In their eyes there was great change that needed to occur before sinners could be welcomed into the loving arms of Jesus. There must be change. No one who ever participated in Jesus' vision of kingdom life ever remained the same. But Jesus never demanded the change *before* he offered acceptance. He offered acceptance, and then the change occurred as a natural result of a grateful and contrite heart.

Imitating Jesus

So how do we imitate Jesus in this? How do we move from becoming an exclusive people to an inclusive people? And how do we become inclusive without relaxing the distinction of the gospel message? Let me offer a few suggestions.

Examine Your Culture

No stratum of society is free of its outcasts. There are always those who are in control, in power, who have more influence than others in the community. Every society, every city, every culture, and every neighborhood has its outsiders, those who aren't welcomed by the mainstream. The first step in becoming like Jesus in welcoming in the outsiders is to examine our own culture or neighborhood and critically reflect upon who is marginalized.

I hesitate to say exactly who they are, for every community is different. If I say "the poor," someone living in a very affluent, gated community may have a tough time finding anyone living at the subsistence level in his or her neighborhood. Having dinner with "Gentiles" and "tax collectors" is a tough sell in America these days. Nevertheless, there are those in our culture, in our towns, in our churches, and in our neighborhoods who are marginalized, disenfranchised, and in need of connecting points with the grace of God as it flows through Jesus. Critical examination of our own culture will help us identify them and sensitize our spirit toward making sure they are included.

Do Not Show Favoritism

It's human nature to join with others of like heart and mind. When I was a teenager our youth leaders continually challenged us about the danger of "cliques," social groups of like-minded teens who were exclusive and condescending. It wasn't long until I came to see that cliques were just as much a problem for adults as they were for teens and that the only difference between a "clique" and a "peer group" was whether or not I was in it. We romanticize the notion that "opposites attract," but studies show time and again that it's commonalities, shared interests, and like-minded viewpoints that keep us together.

If God's heart continually yearns for the outcast, and if his desire is that I become like him and think in the same manner, then it is incumbent on me to embrace everyone I meet as I would a potential friend. In 1 Corinthians 12:22–25, Paul tells us that certain parts of the body are treated with more concern and care than other parts, and his argument isn't just about human anatomy. The widow, the orphan, the oppressed, the outcast, and the "sinner" need just as much care, love, and concern—perhaps more—than those who know God and serve him.

It can't be a matter of pity. God has not called us to offer pity to those who are less fortunate than us. Rather, God calls us to a radical new way of thinking and living. When we, like Jesus, come to the place where we can honestly understand that "he causes his sun to rise on the evil and the good" (Matt. 5:45), and that "there is neither Jew nor Greek, slave nor free, male nor female" (Gal. 3:28), then we will be able to live as he lived and welcome into our presence anyone whom God places before us with no regard for the person's social standing.

Extend the Invitation

Once we have come to a new way of thinking and understand that God wants us to welcome in everyone as a friend, we must then extend the invitation. By "invitation" I don't mean what some traditions call the "altar call." But I mean something more than an invitation to dinner or playing cards. Jesus said to Andrew and Philip, "Come . . . and you will see" (John 1:39), and once they saw, they knew more of who Jesus was and what he wanted for their lives.

This is the kind of invitation I envision—an opportunity to become friends, and to let that friendship lead toward a proclamation of the gospel. It will mean setting aside some time for barbecues that we weren't planning, and for some card games that may interrupt our schedule, and for sitting on my neighbor's front porch while he drinks a beer and asks me about God's will for his life. Many people I know would frown that I would even sit there while he drinks, fearing that my holiness will be compromised by association with him. All the while I'm sipping on some peach tea, and he's asking me why I continually refuse a beer when he offers me one. That is how the conversation leads to Jesus, to kingdom, and to what God wants for his life. The problem was never the beer, or his cigarettes, or his tattoos, or the fact that he's living with a woman he's not married to. His problem is deeper, more foundational. Once I've offered an invitation to him to be in my life and communicated to him that, as a believer in Christ, I have no intention of harassing him about his external issues, he feels safe enough to let me converse with him about the things that matter. Once those internal issues are addressed and his heart is transformed anew by Christ Jesus, then the external issues will follow through the sanctification of the Holy Spirit.

Jesus' ministry was characterized by a welcoming in of the outsiders. In his day they were much different than they are in ours. But every society has those who are marginalized by the mainstream and pushed out by the powerful. If we are to become godly, if we are to imitate Jesus in his spirituality, our task is to embrace these people. We may be ostracized ourselves. We may be marginalized and castigated for our association. But we will be imitating Jesus in doing so and may reply honestly with him, "It is not the healthy who need a doctor, but the sick" (Matt. 9:12).

For Further Reflection

1. Who were the outcasts in Jesus' day?
2. How did Jesus welcome them in?
3. Many of the Jewish leaders of Jesus' day accused him of relaxing the requirements of the Law by associating with these kinds of people. If you were there, what would you have thought about his practice?

4. Why do you suppose Jesus offered acceptance *before* demanding change?
5. Who are the "outcasts" in your neighborhood? In your church? In your school?
6. Who are the kinds of people most folks in your church would never expect to find there?
7. On a scale of 1 to 10, how is your church at reaching out to the outcasts in your community?
8. What could be done to increase the congregation's awareness and involvement in this issue?

■

EIGHT

Fellowship Meals

■JESUS SPENT A LOT OF TIME EATING with a variety of people. He wasn't all that discriminating about whom he shared the table with, for the Gospels show him sharing meals with Pharisees and scribes, tax collectors, and "sinners," in addition to his own disciples. On two separate occasions, he provided the meal for the multitudes (more than five thousand on one occasion and more than four thousand on another), and it's reasonable to assume that they were comprised of all kinds of people from those regions. During his ministry Jesus regularly participated in fellowship meals with people of various socioeconomic and pietistic backgrounds.

It's hard to think of eating as a spiritual discipline. Here in the United States we are continually reminded about our growing obesity levels. Food is omnipresent in our society. It's at the grocery store, the gas station, the hospital, sporting events, weddings, and funerals. Even the local library here in Kissimmee has vending machines in the lobby. Along with the prevalence of food and rising obesity, our culture is obsessed with diet and fitness. Slender celebrities paraded in the media convince us that to be skinny is to be desired, respected, and important, creating for many people a subconscious fear about food. Combine those factors with the spiritual importance Scripture places on both the discipline of fasting[1] and the sin of gluttony,[2] and it becomes difficult to imagine how eating could have fostered spiritual vitality in the life of Jesus and those around him.

We've been considering what, exactly, constituted Jesus' spirituality, examining the things he did on a regular basis that either fostered the power of the Spirit in his life or gave rise to occasions in which he could minister in the Spirit, either through teaching or healing. Jesus' participation in fellowship meals was not simply about his physical nourishment. Neither do I think it was solely about the meal itself. With the exception of the loaves, the fishes, and the bread broken at the Last Supper, the Gospels never describe the food set at Jesus' table. This suggests that the discipline was not in the eating but in the kinds of people Jesus welcomed to the table.

Fellowship meals in our culture are not as prominent as they were in the first century. So before we examine Jesus' habit of sharing fellowship meals with his contemporaries, we must review the purpose and prominence of fellowship meals in the ancient world, particularly in Judaism. Then we will be in a better position to consider the people Jesus ate with, why he was there, and what lessons may be drawn for modern Christian spirituality as a result.

The Importance of Meals in Ancient Culture

The table was a place of friendship and fellowship in antiquity. Meals were shared by those agreeing to covenants, by friends and family in fellowship, and at a variety of religious feast days such as Passover and Pentecost.[3] The table was a place where friends were honored and enemies ridiculed. In the Twenty-third Psalm, David

imagined that Yahweh would prepare him a table in the presence
of his enemies (v. 5), presumably in vindication; and on occasion
the Lord taunted his enemies by threatening to make them food
for the wild beasts and the birds of the air.[4]

In antiquity the table reinforced important ideas of friendship and patronage. Sharing a meal with someone in the ancient
world signaled inclusion into a larger group. It was a rich symbol
of friendship. So wealthy aristocrats invited their wealthy aristo-
cratic friends to their banquets to impress them and solidify their
reputation among the community elites. Being invited to table by
those of higher social standing was a real honor. Estranged friends
and colleagues could be forgiven through an invitation to table
fellowship, and betrayal by one who had shared your table was
a great sign of disrespect.[5] Table fellowship was a deep sign of
friendship, and those who shared the table were friends indeed.
Jesus extended this kind of friendship to people of every social
strata. Bucking a culture that invited only those of like-minded
ideology and social status (with hopes of reciprocity), Jesus shared
the table with all kinds of people, regardless of their importance,
ideology, or social standing.

There was a great concern among the Jews that the table
remain pure. The table was for more than nourishment. The Jewish Mishnah suggests it was for friendship, fellowship, and the
discussion of godly things.[6] Most conscientious Jews of the first
century would not have accepted meals in the homes of Gentiles.
Invitations to pagan feasts (which so often degenerated into drunk-
enness, godless philosophy, and sexual promiscuity) largely would
have been declined. Jews might have recognized the need to invite
the outcasts to their own meals, but they seldom attended feasts
in the homes of Gentiles.[7] Against this background Jesus' indis-
criminate table fellowship with the clean and unclean alike seems
rather offensive. His practice of sharing the table with certain

members of the religious leadership was to be expected. That he spent time at meal with the outcasts (tax collectors and "sinners") was *not* kosher.

Jesus constantly challenged the religious tradition of his day by freely attending *at the homes of others* meals and dinners in his honor. He didn't seem too worried about the holiness problem— that he would become defiled by accepting invitations to table with outcasts. Rather, it was in the context of these meals that Jesus found opportunities for the Spirit to work through him. McMahan puts it best: "The meal, one of humankind's most basic and common practices, was transformed by Jesus into an occasion of divine encounter. It was in the sharing of food and drink that he invited his companions to share in the grace of God."[8]

For the last several decades, scholars have set Jesus' meals against the backdrop of the Greco-Roman *symposia*. The symposium was a group meal, normally consisting of one's friends and loved ones, followed by philosophical discussion and entertainment.[9] Many of the meals Jesus attended in the Gospels ended with discussion or debate, and it's easy to see elements of the symposium in the background. But the symposium is less likely the background for Jesus' activities[10] than is the Old Testament imagery of the great messianic banquet.

Isaiah 25:6–9 depicts a time when God's people share a meal with him on Mount Zion. God had prefigured this by inviting the elders of Israel to feast with him on Mount Sinai (Exod. 24:9–11), and Isaiah predicted the time when God would again graciously invite others to table. The table is set with rich food and drink: "the best of meats and the finest of wines" (Isa. 25:6). Meat wasn't a staple in the average, daily Jewish diet,[11] so the description of fine meat on the table signals festive activity. The meal is spread for God's people, and as they partake in the banquet, Yahweh shares his own delicacy as he feasts on death. He "will swallow up death forever" (v. 8) and remove "the sheet that covers all nations" (v. 7). The gourmet food, however, is not the focus of the banquet.

The main thrust of the great messianic banquet (as it appears in the text of Isaiah) is neither the quality of food spread there nor the bliss that we share in intimate fellowship with God. Rather, the thrust of the promise rests on *who sits at the table*. Three times in these four verses the phrase "all peoples" or "all nations" appears. Not only has God spread a massive banquet, but he also has invited *everyone* to share in it. The universal call to participation then becomes more personal as God calls them "*his* people" (v. 8). The thrust of the messianic banquet is not the food or the act of eating with God but rather the invitation for anyone and everyone to come and sit at God's table.

This, I suggest, is the background for table fellowship events in Jesus' ministry. Jesus was not reticent to attend feasts with tax collectors and "sinners" (though he was called "a glutton and a drunkard" for doing so; Matt. 11:19), for everyone is welcome at the table. Neither did he spurn the invitation to dinner with Pharisees, for again, everyone is welcome at the table. Several of Jesus' comments have the great messianic banquet imagery in mind. For instance, Jesus praised the faith of the centurion by saying, "I say to you that many will come from the east and the west, and will take their places at the feast with Abraham, Isaac and Jacob in the kingdom of heaven" (Matt. 8:11). Those coming to "the feast" come from east and west (a colloquial way of saying "all peoples"), and take "their places," as if they had been appointed to them. On another occasion, at a dinner in the home of a prominent Pharisee, one of the guests proclaimed, "Blessed is the man who will eat at the feast in the kingdom of God" (Luke 14:15). Jesus responded to this man's self-appointed blessing by telling a parable of a great banquet that eventually involved the servants recruiting attendees from the streets, the alleys, and the outer reaches of civilized culture to make sure that the banquet was full (Luke 14:23). Jesus' comments demonstrate that he understood the main thrust of Isaiah's messianic banquet to be the inclusion of the outsiders, and his practice of meal-sharing with people from all ideologies and social levels fleshes out his understanding of Scripture and provided him significant opportunities for the Spirit to work through him.

With Whom Is Jesus Eating?

The striking thing about Jesus' discipline of meal-sharing was that he invited *everyone* to table with him. He wasn't picky about whom he invited to table. The Gospels portray him sharing meals with Pharisees, tax collectors and "sinners," and his disciples. On a couple of occasions, he created a meal in the open countryside with the masses. More striking still is that in most of the instances in which he shared a meal with others, Jesus ate in their homes, contrary to the custom of many concerned with holiness in his day.

Pharisees

On several occasions we find Jesus eating in the home of Pharisees. My parents took me to church when I was two weeks old, and from that time on, most of what I heard in church about the Pharisees involved their being the hated enemies of Jesus. There were certainly Pharisees who were out to get him, and as a group they appear as the main antagonists in Jesus' ministry. But not all of the Pharisees were hostile toward Jesus. Nicodemus was a Pharisee and member of the ruling council in Jerusalem. He came to see Jesus to learn more about his teachings, challenged the Sanhedrin to act fairly in regard to Jesus' situation, and helped care for his body after the crucifixion.[12] There were some Pharisees who were genuinely concerned for Jesus' well-being. Once when Jesus planned to go through Samaria (a route that would have taken

him near the southern edge of Tiberias, where Herod's palace lay)
a group of Pharisees cautioned Jesus about taking that route.[13]
Herod already had put John the Baptist to death and then had
begun seeking an audience with Jesus. If he caught up with Jesus,
the outcome was predictable. Though Jesus didn't think much of
the threat,[14] this group of Pharisees in Jesus' company were genuinely concerned for him.

Luke presents Jesus spending time at table with the Pharisees.
The first occasion took place in Galilee in the home of a Pharisee named Simon. He had invited Jesus to dinner in his home
(7:36), and Jesus accepted. It was in Simon's home that the sinful
woman came to anoint Jesus with the expensive perfume, prompting Simon's objection and Jesus' statement about her response to
God's grace. On another occasion Jesus was invited by another
Pharisee, this one unnamed, to have dinner in his home, and
Luke tells us that Jesus went. Conversation wasn't so pleasant during this meal, as the host Pharisee questioned Jesus about his lack
of ceremonial washings (think "Pharisaic tradition"). Jesus challenged them in a number of ways about their traditions, prompting one of the experts in the Law to wittingly say, "Teacher, when
you say these things, you insult us" (11:45). The meeting did not
end well (Luke says they "began to oppose him fiercely" and bar-
rage him with trick questions, 11:53–54), but Jesus spoke the word
of God to them nonetheless. This would not have been possible
had he not accepted the invitation to table fellowship. The third
instance occurred in the home of a prominent Pharisee (14:1–24).
Luke tells us only that Jesus had gone there to eat, presumably
because he was again invited. The meal became the setting for the
healing of a man with dropsy, some counsel from Jesus regarding
the importance that Pharisees placed on their meals, and the parable about the great messianic banquet (see earlier discussion).

Jesus was not always antagonistic toward the Pharisees. He

spent time with them, as he did with other groups. Sure, they challenged him, and he spoke the truth to them. But there's a reason that they kept inviting him to dinner. Some of them challenged him openly in the synagogues, but others chose to seek a hearing before offering their questions. Still others were sympathetic toward him and wanted to participate in what God might have been doing in Jesus' ministry. Whatever their reasons, Jesus ate with them when he was invited, and accepting the invitations placed him in a unique position to allow the Spirit of God to flow through him—in a proper challenge of the Pharisees' traditions—and speak the truth of God to them.

Tax Collectors and "Sinners"

We expect to find Jesus having table fellowship with the Jewish leadership. Indeed, that is what *they* expected.[15] But Jesus also shared the table with the outcasts, particularly tax collectors and "sinners." The Gospels place him in the home of the tax collector Matthew, sharing a banquet with "a large crowd of tax collectors" (Luke 5:29) and "sinners" (Matt. 9:10). Similarly, the calling of the chief tax collector Zacchaeus resulted in a meal (Luke 19:1–10). No meal is mentioned explicitly, but contextual clues in Luke's gospel suggest it. Luke already had mentioned the grumbling of the Pharisees in regard to Jesus eating with tax collectors and "sinners" (15:1–2), and the calling of the tax collector Matthew ended in table fellowship, which became the occasion for the Pharisees' objection that Jesus ate with the likes of them.[16] So here again we have Jesus in the home of a tax collector, followed by a rebuke that "he has gone to be the guest of a 'sinner'" (Luke 19:7). It seems that table fellowship is in view in the home of Zacchaeus.[17]

Jesus' table fellowship with the tax collectors and "sinners" became the setting for the parables of the lost in Luke 15. The Pharisees and the teachers of the Law "muttered" about his practice of eating with them (v. 2). The word translated "muttered" in the NIV, has the sense of grumbling behind one's back, and Luke suggests that they were doing so constantly.[18] Jesus' response was to tell three parables, each involving something lost being found or coming back and highlighting the great joy that results. These parables were not told to the tax collectors and "sinners" but rather told to the Pharisees and teachers of the Law in response to their accusation that he shared the table with the unclean. Jesus made no apologies for having table fellowship with the outcasts, and he offered a challenge to the Pharisees and scribes to repent themselves and come into the party (Luke 15:28).[19]

Jesus refused to turn away those who invited him to the table. As he fleshed out the great messianic banquet, everyone was welcome to sit down and eat with him. The Jewish leaders expected to be there. They probably never considered that the Messiah might share the table with tax collectors and "sinners." By doing so, and by making this a regular part of his discipline, Jesus was afforded significant teaching opportunities that allowed the Spirit to do the work of conviction through Jesus' challenge to the Pharisees, and he fulfilled a prophecy given by the Spirit of the Lord.

The Disciples

While Jesus had table fellowship with Pharisees, tax collectors, and "sinners," he did not forsake his closest companions to do so. Jesus shared the table with his disciples on a number of occasions. Given that they spent nearly every day together for almost three years, it was more of a regular occurrence than the evidence will document. Nevertheless, the Gospels record a number of statements about Jesus' meal-sharing with his disciples.

Early in his ministry Jesus spent time in the home of Peter's mother-in-law. She had been ill with a fever (the kind that doesn't go away with an aspirin), and Jesus went there to heal her. Once she was well enough to get out of bed, she began to "wait on them" (Mark 1:31). The word actually means "serve" and brings the connotation of meal preparation.[20] The Twelve hadn't been called yet, but clearly this was a meal with some of his disciples and closest followers. The same also was true in the home of Mary and Martha. Martha had "opened her home to him" (Luke 10:38), and in the midst of the preparations that had to be made, she grew frustrated with her sister and asked Jesus to intercede on her behalf (Luke 10:40). The context of the setting suggests that she was preparing for a meal that Jesus would share with his closest friends and disciples.[21]

During the final week of his life, a dinner was given for Jesus in the home of Simon the Leper.[22] Among the invited guests were Simon, Mary, Martha, Lazarus, and the Twelve, including Judas. This meal became the occasion for Mary to anoint Jesus' body for burial and the objection by Judas that the perfume could have been sold and the money used to help the poor. The result was Jesus' proclamation that Mary's anointing of him would be told wherever the gospel was preached. For two thousand years, that story has been told, and it took place in the setting of Jesus' table fellowship with his closest friends.

During that final week, Jesus also shared in an extensive Passover meal with his disciples that became the occasion for his monologue about the ministry of the Spirit[23] and the institution of the sacrament of the Lord's Supper. Once again, we find significant spiritual stuff taking place in the context of meal settings.

I largely have been unconcerned with Jesus' postresurrection activities. We've been examining the things he did as a human being to foster the power of the Spirit in his life and provide opportunities for ministry in the Spirit. After the resurrection Jesus appeared in a changed, glorified body. What he did in his glorified state, while important, doesn't help us to understand and imitate his earthly discipline. But I want to mention here two occasions when, even after his resurrection, Jesus found it worthwhile to spend time eating with his disciples. The first occurred in conjunction with the miraculous catch of fish. John simply tells us that "when they had finished eating" Jesus began to question Peter about his true loyalties (John 21:1–19). Luke mentions that on another occasion Jesus shared an extensive meal with two disciples on the road to Emmaus. At first the two didn't recognize him, but "when he was at the table with them," he broke the bread, gave thanks, and gave it to them—and then they recognized him (Luke 24:13–35; cf. Mark 16:12–13). Did they see the scars on his hands as he handed them the bread? Or did they recognize the *way* he gave thanks and broke the bread as indicative of Jesus' practice? Whatever the case, Jesus found it worthwhile to spend time at table with his disciples even after his resurrection, suggesting its importance to him.

The Crowds

It's hard to think about Jesus having table fellowship with crowds, in the same way it might be difficult to have an elegant meal with a friend at the state fair. Yet on two occasions Jesus *created* a meal for the multitudes out of what amounted to nothing at all. With the feeding of the five thousand,[24] he miraculously multiplied five small loaves of bread and two fish. Jesus gave thanks, broke the bread, and distributed it to the disciples. They all ate, including Jesus. Thus, he shared a meal, not only with his disciples, but also with the multitudes. The same scenario played itself out in the feeding of the four thousand,[25] when seven small loaves and a few fish were multiplied to feed the crowd. Once again, Jesus gave thanks, broke the bread, distributed it, and "they all ate and were satisfied" (Matt. 15:37). As significant a spiritual event as the multiplication of the food was, both events prompted significant teaching on Jesus' part to those who wanted more (John 6:25–59) and to the disciples who were to be on guard against "the yeast of the Pharisees" (Matt. 16:5–12; Mark

8:14–21; Luke 12:1). Table fellowship afforded Jesus some significant opportunities to do spiritual ministry, even with the crowds.

Enacting the Messianic Banquet

The meals we eat and the people we share them with say a great deal about our character. My family and I live in central Florida, home to Disney World, Universal Studios, and some of the world's best beaches. We previously lived in the Midwest, and we have many friends who visit us during their vacations here. No matter who comes, we always try to share a meal with our guests. We treat them to a few local hotspots, vestiges of local Floridian culture, but the emphasis is less on the meal than on sharing time with our friends and catching up on life.

Holiday festivals were like that in my childhood home. For most major holidays (Christmas, New Year's, Thanksgiving, and Easter), the entire family gathered at my grandfather's house to celebrate. There was always plenty of food (what Veronika Grimm calls "prestige food"[26]) and never a shortage of leftovers. The table was never closed, but always open to college mates who needed a surrogate family on these holidays. My wife and I have attempted to practice this same kind of open-meal policy around the holidays. We live too far away from our immediate families to travel home for Thanksgiving, so we have attempted to become a surrogate family for those on campus who are in the same situation.

I realize this seems reminiscent of Jesus eating with his disciples and a bit like Romans sharing meals with their friends. But we've also shared a meal or two with a tax collector and "sinner." Our neighbors are not believers, at least not by any evangelical standards. We've shared meals with them on numerous occasions—for special occasions and ordinary ones, in the backyard, on the front porch, in their home and in ours. The first time we invited them to church with us it was Easter Sunday, and we treated them to a meal at our favorite local restaurant. I'm no first-century Roman, and I've never participated in a *symposium*, but I do find that mealtime has created some of the most meaningful conversations we've had with our neighbors about things of the kingdom.

This has meant that sometimes I've had to eat some things I didn't care for. I find in Jesus' discipline of table fellowship that the food itself isn't the main focus of the meal. In fact, everything I see in Jesus' teaching suggests that food itself is not a matter of holiness as God defines it. As he sent them out to preach, Jesus told his disciples to eat whatever was set before them (Luke 10:7–8) and reminded those challenging him about certain foods being unclean that God has equipped the body with a natural cleansing system, ensuring that in the end all food is clean (Mark 7:19).[27] Many evangelicals imitate the Pharisees more than they do Jesus by declaring that certain kinds of food and drink make a person ungodly. We would do well to fully explore Jesus' counsel that nothing I put in my mouth makes me unclean (Matt. 15:11, 17–20; Mark 7:14–19).

For Jesus, the main thrust of the meal was not the food. As we examine Jesus' discipline of sharing the table, it becomes clear that for him the main point is *whom we invite to the table*. Jesus welcomed everyone, not just those like him. He never expected reciprocity, like so many in the first century; and he never gave much credence to social strata or hierarchical structures around the table. He certainly never set out different qualities and quantities of food for the more important guests.[28] Jesus welcomed them all in, fleshing out Isaiah's messianic banquet with its "all peoples" motif in ways that his Jewish contemporaries did not. "Jesus' table-fellowship turns the world upside down for he welcomes anyone, especially sinners and the unclean, to eat with him anywhere and at anytime."[29] Perhaps it is time for Christians in the modern world to spend a little less time with our own, expecting reciprocity in our meal-sharing, and to take Jesus' advice seriously to "invite the poor, the crippled, the lame, the blind" (Luke 14:13). The conversations will naturally turn to kingdom-minded things as they did in Jesus' ministry, and, in the Spirit, the message of the grace and love and welcome of Jesus will flow through us into the hearing of those who need the church's welcome.

For Further Reflection

1. Describe the importance that food has had in your family and your culture.
2. When your family has a sumptuous meal, with whom do you normally eat?
3. With whom did Jesus eat?
4. Describe the importance of fellowship meals in the first-century Greco-Roman world.
5. What place did fellowship meals have among the Jews?
6. Why were Jews in Jesus' day so reluctant to share meals with Gentiles and outcasts?
7. How did Jesus break from the traditions of the religious leaders in his eating habits?
8. If Jesus were here today, what traditions do you think he might call into question with his eating habits? What modern practices (among modern believers) do you think he might challenge in this area?
9. Consider Jesus' statement: "What goes into a man's mouth does not make him 'unclean'" (Matt. 15:11; cf. Matt. 15:17–20; Mark 7:14–19). What relevance does that have today? Can you think of any situations in which that principle might apply?
10. As you read this chapter, whom did you find yourself wishing you could invite to your next meal?

■

NINE

Evangelism and Proclamation

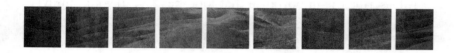

■NEW TESTAMENT SCHOLARS DISAGREE on just about everything imaginable. They disagree about who actually wrote the Gospels, whether the four canonical gospels are authoritative, the nature of Jesus' ministry, whether Jesus knew his death would atone for the sins of the world, whether or not he knew about his death in advance, and whether or not he believed he would be vindicated in resurrection. In all of their simplicity, the ancient sources are complex and full of nuance and meaning, making for disagreement and lack of consensus on many issues. But one thing almost all New Testament scholars agree on is that Jesus came preaching the arrival of the kingdom of God.

We've been searching the Gospels for descriptions of Jesus' daily routine in an attempt to uncover the nature of his everyday spirituality. Certainly, his proclamation of the kingdom deserves attention in our study, for the proclamation of the kingdom was at the heart and focus of his ministry. This chapter is not a discussion of homiletics—that is, Jesus' preaching style. He used various types of illustrations from nature, Scripture, first-century politics, and props available to him at the moment. Jesus' use of rhetorical devices (simile, pun, metaphor, chiasmus, proverbs, parallelism, etc.) is adequately treated elsewhere,[1] and on that topic I could do no better. I'm concerned less with what made Jesus a great communicator and more with the prominence that proclamation of God's kingdom occupied in his personal life and ministry.

The Gospels portray Jesus preaching everywhere he went, and whether he approached the people in the temple or the synagogues, or whether they gathered around him in the countryside and on the mountain, one thing that he was disciplined about was the ministry of proclamation. But it's not enough to say that Jesus ran around the Galilean and Judean countryside preaching. What did he say? What were the consistent themes in his message? Once we've seen Jesus' discipline of proclaiming the good news, I will contrast that with the assumptions made in modern Christianity about what preaching really involves. This will not be easy, for we will have to challenge some long-standing traditional values. I hope that what you find here, though it be challenging, is biblical, accurate, and kingdom-minded.

Jesus the Herald

One of the most frequent activities Jesus engaged in was preaching. Of course, by "preaching" I don't mean that he wore a three-piece polyester suit, carried a leather-bound Torah under his arm, and pounded the pulpit in the synagogue, screaming at the top of his lungs. The *preaching* word group used to describe Jesus' activity draws upon the work of the Roman herald. In the days before e-mail, news crews, and presidential advance teams, a king's arrival in a particular city was preceded by a herald, someone who went ahead and prepared the way for the king's arrival. "The king is coming" was the thrust of the message. The herald also delivered official announcements to the populace.[2] Mark seems to present John the

Baptist serving this role in advance of Jesus' coming. After quoting from Isaiah that God would send a messenger ahead of the Messiah to prepare for his arrival, the next words from Mark after the quote are, "And so John came" baptizing and preaching (Mark 1:4; cf. Isa. 40:3). John was a herald of the coming Messiah. Jesus also was a herald, announcing the coming (or arrival) of the kingdom of God.[3]

Heralding the Kingdom

From the very outset, Jesus' message was characterized by the announcement of the coming—or arrival—of the kingdom of God. I make a distinction between the "coming" and the "arrival" of the kingdom of God because that is precisely what the Gospels indicate—both the imminence (or nearness) of the kingdom *and* its arrival in the person and ministry of Jesus. The first recorded statement that Mark gives of Jesus' preaching offers an apt illustration of the problem: "The time has come. . . . The kingdom of God is near" (Mark 1:15). Has the kingdom "come" or is it "near"? While running the risk of befuddling the argument, I must simply answer, yes. The biblical evidence runs both ways. At times Jesus spoke as if the kingdom had already arrived. Answering questions about his exorcisms, he replied, "If I drive out demons by the finger of God, then the kingdom of God has come to you" (Luke 11:20; cf. Matt. 12:28). On another occasion he answered the Pharisees' question about the arrival of the kingdom with a straightforward "the kingdom of God is within you" (Luke 17:21), or "within your reach."[4] These statements would suggest that as Jesus appears, so does the kingdom. But at other times, Jesus spoke as if the kingdom would reach its fulfillment in the future. He taught his disciples to pray for the advent of God's kingdom (Matt. 6:10; Luke 11:2) and indicated at the Last Supper that he would not drink the final cup "until the kingdom of God comes" (Luke 22:18). The biblical data presents Jesus speaking both ways, at times suggesting the kingdom had already come and at other times hinting at the kingdom's arrival in the future.[5] How can we make sense of this?

Part of the solution lies in the different perceptions of time and space between people of the twenty-first century and those living two thousand years ago. We live in an atomistic culture. We're aware that matter is made of atoms (protons, neutrons, electrons) and that there are further divisions of these particles (e.g., quarks) that have yet to be fully understood. We think in very minute ("atomistic") categories. We reckon time in minutes and seconds, and trace our family trees in linear, exact fashion. These are the trappings of the Western mind. The ancient, Eastern mind ran more along broader categories. Consider how differently people in the Scriptures speak of time: "about the third hour" (Matt. 20:3), "very early in the morning" (Mark 15:1), and "Jesus himself was about thirty years old" (Luke 3:23). These are much more general, less exact ways of reckoning time. Genealogies often were construed politically or theologically rather than constructed along exact parentage,[6] and anyone connected to the bloodline could be considered a relative or a "father."[7] They were much more general and categorical than our own genealogical records. The Western mind tends to look at the conflicting statements about the coming of the kingdom as grounds for discrepancy. "How can it have arrived but yet still only be near?" If we back away from the text and consider Jesus' statements in their whole, we will find that the kingdom comes *with Jesus*—both in his person and in the ministry he inaugurated. When Jesus shows up, so does the kingdom. But it is only the beginning, and there is much more to it than just his presence.

Defining the Kingdom

I've always struggled to know how to define the "kingdom of God," and judging by the way scholars, preachers, and theologians talk about it, I'm not the only one. Is the kingdom of God the church? Is it a land-based kingdom, with borders, a palace, and a king—a restored Israel where God anoints his Davidic-type warrior to reign as David did millennia ago? Is it a concept or a way of thinking, a way of being God's people in the midst of a godless world? Interestingly, I find that Jesus wasn't all that concerned about defining the phrase "kingdom of God/heaven." He was constantly talking about the kingdom, not in terms of what it *is*, but always in terms of what it is *like*. He wasn't concerned to debate the definition of the kingdom. Either his hearers already had a shared understanding of it, or he didn't feel that defining it was necessary. Instead, Jesus told parables indicating the *qualities* or *properties* of God's kingdom. The kingdom of heaven is like a grain of mustard growing to immense proportions, a farmer recklessly slinging seed, a dragnet that catches all kinds of fish, a landowner hiring workers to tend his vineyard, and bridesmaids waiting anxiously for the return of the bridegroom.[8]

The classic definition of the kingdom of God has been "the place where God rules," and to a large extent, that's a good definition. But it has largely left me hanging, unable to clearly define exactly where God *does* rule. Is it in my heart, in my mind, or in heaven?

In an attempt to get my mind in order and wrap my thinking biblically around the concept of the kingdom of God, I've begun thinking of it in terms given by the prophet Micah. While making his legal case against Israel for her disobedience against Yahweh, Micah decried the many gestures that might be attempted to abate their punishment. Were they to offer it, the Lord would not be pleased with the sacrifice of rams, or even the firstborn of a man's children. Micah articulates exactly what God is looking for: "He has showed you, O man, what is good. And what does the LORD require of you? To act justly and to love mercy and to walk humbly with your God" (Mic. 6:8). Three traits sum up all that God wants from his people: justice, mercy, and righteousness. These are the essence of the kingdom, and where you find them at work in God's way for God's purposes, there you find God's rule and kingdom.

Micah describes the first trait God desires in his people with the phrase "act justly" (literally, "do justice"). Justice has social ramifications.[9] It involves setting things right. God's kingdom is characterized by God's people behaving amicably toward one another. Justice is not only proactive but at times will need to be reactive. Bad things happen, and when they do, justice must be established and maintained. This involves making sure that the weak and the oppressed get a fair shake, that neighbors act fairly in their business dealings with one another, and that the oppressor is adequately prosecuted.

"Mercy" translates a rich word in Old Testament literature: ḥesed. It conveys the ideas of compassion, mercy, and authentic love, both toward God and toward others. Ḥesed was the backbone of the covenant, and only when one offered it to another human being was that person prepared to receive it from God.[10] "Mercy," "compassion," "loving-kindness," and even "loyalty" are adequate words used to translate this term.[11] Jesus chided the Pharisees for failing to demonstrate mercy when he said, "They tie up heavy loads and put them on men's shoulders, but they themselves are not willing to lift a finger to move them" (Matt. 23:4). When God's people demonstrate mercy and compassion toward one another, there God is having his way. Mercy is set in apposition to justice— in tandem even—for one must not outrun the other. When justice and mercy are held in perfect balance, so are relations with community and God.

The phrase "to walk humbly with your God" implies a sense of diligence and careful observation regarding our relationship with him. God's kingdom is not having its full effect wherever God's people are not in right relationship with him. *Righteousness* is an adequate term to describe the concept. Righteousness involves knowing and doing what God wants done, saying what he wants said, and representing him in a real and honest way with a holy lifestyle plainly visible to those who know us. Jesus' vision of the kingdom requires the kind of righteousness that outshines that of the Jewish leadership[12] and that we become, by our holiness, salt and light in a dark and putrid world.[13] Paul would later carry on Jesus' work, proclaiming both the gracious gift of God in making men righteous[14] and an ethical demand for righteous living in response.[15]

This threefold expression—justice, mercy, righteousness—seems to adequately sum up the essence of the kingdom in terms of right relations with God and neighbor. Jesus made several statements along this line, including the Great Commandment (to "love God" and "love your neighbor"; Matt. 22:37–40; Mark 12:29–31) and the criticism of the Pharisees that they had focused too much on the inconsequential and not enough on the "more important matters of the law—justice, mercy and faithfulness" (Matt. 23:23).

I have given this lengthy digression on Jesus' preaching of the kingdom, and exactly what "kingdom" means, to set the stage for Jesus' discipline of proclamation. Jesus spent much of his time proclaiming the message that the kingdom had come (and was coming still). Understanding what he said and how often he said it will help us to evaluate our own discipline of proclaiming what God wants from his people. Jesus did not come to inaugurate a privatized religion, a way of relating to God in isolation. He also shied away from disputes about legalistic righteousness and Torah minutiae, which only exacerbated the divide between the "clean" and the "unclean" and were not concerned with compassion and love. Instead, he came to establish a redeemed community, to help the Father fashion for himself a holy people who behaved rightly toward one another—in mercy and justice.

Jesus' Practice of Preaching

From the first moments of Jesus' ministry, his desire was for the proclamation of the kingdom. Mark 1:14 notes that after John the Baptist was put in prison, Jesus went to Galilee and began to preach, and from that point forward proclamation and evangelism ("telling the good news") became the focal point of his ministry. Sure, there were miracles, healings, and exorcisms. But these were not the reason that he came. Time and time again Jesus made it clear to his disciples that his desire was to preach and teach the people.

He preached first and foremost in the synagogue. The number of references to Jesus preaching in the synagogue indicates that it was a favored place for him. He began his ministry by preaching in the synagogues in Galilee[16] and made the synagogue one of the first (if not *the* first) places he proclaimed the message of the kingdom in a given area. His response to the pressing crowds (and Peter's accusation that he was ignoring them) was to boldly proclaim, "Let us go somewhere else—to the nearby villages—so I can preach there also. That is why I have come" (Mark 1:38; cf. Luke 4:42–44). The Gospels consistently portray Jesus teaching in the synagogues, gaining a hearing for his message about God's work and activity among his people.[17] Given that any qualified male could deliver the exposition of the sermon, Jesus probably found the synagogue a ready-made venue for making connections between God's promises to Israel and their fulfillment in his own ministry. His proclamation in the synagogue afforded him opportunities to heal the infirm,[18] defend himself against accusations resulting from those healings,[19] and establish himself among the people as one who had authority.[20]

But the synagogue was not the only place that Jesus found occasion to preach. He regularly made trips to the Jerusalem temple for the Jewish feasts and there seized the opportunity to address the gathering crowds. Jesus once indicated to his brothers that he would not attend the Feast of Tabernacles, mostly to rebut their taunting that he make a public spectacle of himself and his ministry. Once their temptation had passed, Jesus quietly attended the feast (John 7:1–10). Midway through the feast, he went to the temple courts and began to teach. His themes were centered mostly on his identity as the Messiah,[21] the integrity of the Jewish leaders[22] and their challenges to his benevolent acts of kindness.[23] John later presents Jesus teaching in Solomon's Colonnade during the Feast of Dedication, where both the antagonism of the Jewish leaders and the bewilderment of the people are again on display.[24] The Jewish temple was a major icon for Israel, so Jesus spent a great deal of time there in the days leading up to his arrest. The Synoptics tell us that during the final week of his life, Jesus spent his days teaching in the temple.[25] This became the setting for Jesus' proclamation of his identity[26] and ministry and his honest appraisal of the Jewish leaders' performance as wicked tenants of Yahweh's vineyard.[27]

Jesus' proclamation of the arrival of God's kingdom couldn't be confined to the Jewish institutions of synagogue and temple, however. Jesus found occasion to address the burgeoning crowds whenever the opportunities presented themselves. He addressed them on the shore of the Sea of Galilee,[28] in the home,[29] on the side of a mountain,[30] on a large open plain,[31] and in several other venues.[32] Jesus did not need the porch in the temple or the seat of Moses in the synagogue to proclaim his message. He proclaimed it anywhere people would listen and to anyone who had an interest.

The prominence of the spoken word in Jesus' ministry suggests that in this area we may finally be able to arrive at a glimpse of Jesus' giftedness in the Spirit. Paul would later teach that those who are indwelt by the Spirit have been gifted by the Spirit for the edification of God's people.[33] Hebrews 12:2 describes Jesus as the prototype or "archetype" of our own experience, which suggests that having been indwelt by the Spirit of God Jesus also would

have been gifted by the Spirit for his ministry. From the statements that Jesus made and his relentless activity in proclaiming
the kingdom's arrival and availability to all men, it seems that
Jesus couldn't *not* preach. His skill as a rhetorician complemented
his passion to proclaim the gospel, making him a powerful communicator of the Spirit's truth about God's kingdom. This is the
classic definition of a spiritual gift, and it seems that, at least in
this area, Jesus may have been spiritually gifted.

The Training of the Disciples

The proclamation of the kingdom of God and its ethical
implications was vitally important to Jesus' ministry and his spirituality. Knowing that the time would come when he would no
longer be physically able to proclaim the message of the kingdom,
he trained his disciples to carry on his work, both during his own
ministry and after his departure. Being in his presence daily was
a substantial training in itself. But the Gospels also present to us
two specific occasions when Jesus trained his disciples to carry on
his work of proclaiming the good news.

From among his many disciples, Jesus selected twelve men for
greater responsibility in furthering his ministry and the kingdom
of God. Mark tells us that when he chose these twelve, he designated them "apostles," and that he called them "that he might
send them out to preach" (Mark 3:14). In the midst of his ministry in Galilee, Jesus took some time to train them and then send
them out. Their message was in line with his own: "The kingdom
of heaven is near" (or, "has arrived," Matt. 10:7).

Jesus' training was simple, and to imitate him I will not bela-
bor the points here but rather highlight the overarching themes.
Extensive treatment of Jesus' effort to train his disciples for kingdom proclamation has been undertaken by others more compe-
tently than I could offer here.[34] The disciples' mission (presented

in Matthew 10) was simple: they were to go first to the lost sheep of Israel, proclaiming the message of the kingdom's arrival.[35] As they did so, they were to trust in God's provision. As workers in God's kingdom, they were entitled to fair compensation and could be assured that God would take care of them in their journeys. Therefore, they were to take no extra supplies but were to trust that God would provide them with gracious hosts receptive to their message.[36] Jesus prepared them to expect opposition to the message, both from the Jewish authorities in the synagogues and from among their own family members.[37] Jesus encouraged them, in the strongest possible terms (those of divine retribution), to remain faithful to him in the face of imminent persecution.[38]

The Gospels tell us nothing of the results of the preaching tour of the Twelve. Evidently there must have been some success, for during the latter part of his ministry in Galilee, as Jesus was approaching Jerusalem, he pulled together seventy-two disciples from among the larger crowd and trained them for the same purpose (Luke 10:1–16). Jesus' training of the seventy-two is in many ways similar to the training of the Twelve. Jesus sent them out two by two[39] to preach the arrival of the kingdom of God. As they went along, they were to trust that God would again provide them with gracious hosts and food to eat during their stay. He prepared them for opposition, noting the impending doom awaiting anyone who rejected them, for their rejection was ultimately rejection of Jesus and his Father. The training speech is remarkably similar in thematic content to his training of the Twelve, and while scholars hasten to suggest that one or more of the evangelists has either abridged or embellished the oral tradition on this one, I tend to agree with Hughes Oliphant Old that this sermon was probably one that Jesus used often in his training.[40]

Two things need to be said in order to set the stage for the work that follows. First, Jesus' training of his disciples to proclaim the message of the kingdom in an attempt to win converts appears as something new on the Jewish historical scene. Scot McKnight has demonstrated that there is no evidence in the extant literature of any mass program on the part of the Jewish leaders to evangelize the nations and win converts to Judaism from among the Gentiles in the days prior to the ministry of Jesus.[41] There was goodwill toward Gentiles and a willingness to accommodate them if they expressed interest in the Jewish faith, but there was no comprehensive plan for systematically presenting them with the message of Yahweh's saving grace. There was an expectation that the Gentiles would flock toward the temple at the Messiah's appearing, rendering any evangelistic effort pointless.[42] Second, the modern church must not imitate the Judaism of the second-temple period, hoping that if we appease nonbelievers enough they will flock to our churches and there find salvation. Erecting user-friendly buildings in strategic, growing locations is not enough, any more than erecting the temple was a catalyst for any major influx of Gentiles. Jesus took the message to the people, and his discipline of proclamation calls for imitation.

After Jesus' ascension, the disciples carried on his work of proclaiming the in-breaking of the kingdom of God. The book of Acts is peppered with speech after speech in which the apostles (particularly Peter, John, and Paul) proclaimed the message that God's kingdom had come in the ministry of Jesus. Not only did they imitate Jesus' proclamation of the gospel, but they also trained their own disciples to do so. Luke presents men such as Stephen (Acts 6:8–7:53), Philip (Acts 8:26–40), and Barnabas (Acts 13:1–3; 15:36–41) as having the necessary skills, opportunity, and passion to proclaim the gospel message, even under less-than-favorable circumstances.

Proclaiming the Timeless Kingdom in the Modern World

Jesus believed it was his own mission to preach the arrival of the kingdom, and he thought it vital to train his disciples to carry on this work after his departure. They, in turn, found it important enough to train their own disciples, resulting in the succession of preaching throughout church history into the modern era. After this extensive (though not thorough) review of Jesus' practice of proclaiming God's kingdom, it's time now to pause for some reflection on how Jesus' discipline affects our own spiritual practice of evangelism.

Jesus Was Passionate About Proclaiming the Kingdom

When we peruse the Gospels, we find Jesus proclaiming the arrival (and still arriving) kingdom of God at every turn. He was passionate about proclaiming the good news that God would now, in a new way, "release the oppressed" (Luke 4:18) as he had so many times before in other ways. He was passionate about calling men and women to live in the kingdom the way God had always intended—in ways that promote loving-kindness to one another, establish justice in the world, and foster right living with God. This essence of the kingdom—justice, mercy, and righteousness—was the core of his teaching in the synagogue, in the temple, and anywhere he taught the crowds. A kingdom movement without the proclamation of the arrival and continued manifestation of God's kingdom was foreign to Jesus' thinking. In this area the words of Jeremiah ring just as true for Jesus (though, without the complaining): "His word is in my heart like a fire, a fire shut up in my bones. I am weary of holding it in; indeed, I cannot" (Jer. 20:9).

So many times the famous line (often attributed to St. Francis of Assisi, though he never actually made the statement) is brought forward in conjunction with proclamation and evangelism: "Preach the gospel, and if necessary, use words." This statement is often quoted to suggest that it's possible to preach the gospel and never utter a word. The implication is that people will come to know the gospel by the way we live. The good deeds of the Jews were known among the Gentiles, and Peter encourages us to "live such good lives among the pagans that, though they accuse you of doing wrong, they may see your good deeds and glorify God on the day he visits us" (1 Peter 2:12). For those who struggle to speak the truth to nonbelievers, "lifestyle evangelism" can be a genuine form of witness. But lifestyle evangelism is not a substitute for proclamation. Lifestyle evangelism uses godly living as an attractant *that naturally leads to proclamation of the Word.*[43] Quiet, godly living must be balanced with Paul's contention that unbelievers cannot place faith in Christ if they've never heard of him and that they can't hear of him unless someone *speaks* about him (Rom. 10:14–15).

Jesus Couldn't Convince Everyone

Jesus passionately preached the arrival of the kingdom, and while participation in that kingdom was available to everyone, there were some who simply refused to take him up on his offer. The rich young ruler is a case in point,[44] but not the only one. There were Jewish leaders[45] and Galilean peasants[46] who refused to join him even after hearing his message of inclusion, and at least once he likened them to children pouting in the marketplace, refusing to play with their friends.[47] He denounced cities such as Korazin, Bethsaida, and Capernaum for rejecting him.[48] Even in his hometown of Nazareth the result of his kingdom message was a belligerent attempt to throw him off a high cliff.[49] Jesus, crafty public speaker that he was, couldn't persuade everyone to join his cause.

Evangelism frustrates me. I've always been evangelistically minded. By that I mean that I constantly think about the fact that my neighbors need to know the saving grace of God. I worry that some of my family members have yet to embrace the kingdom, and I fret about what I'm supposed to do with the woman seated next to me on a plane. Do I create a conversation about whether she knows Jesus or simply allow conversation to lead us there? Evangelism is frequently on my mind. But I've never been good at it. My father is a natural salesman, but apparently that gift doesn't run in the bloodline. I was taught a number of evangelistic techniques in my Bible college training, and I've used several of them, but always with minimal levels of success. To be honest, the prepackaged forms have always felt rigid, cold, and uncomfortable. So I fail a lot in my attempts at sharing the kingdom. I know about grace and love, but my temperament so easily focuses on judgment and personal responsibility. I've never liked the "cold call" (knocking on people's doors unannounced), because (1) cultic groups frequently do this in my neighborhood and (2) I wouldn't appreciate someone treating me the same way ("as you would have them do to you" [Luke 6:31]). I've found that mass evangelistic campaigns often provide little or no connection to the local church once conversion occurs, creating little hope for lasting transformation.

I suspect that sharing the gospel of the kingdom is more organic and less "cookie-cutter" than I was taught. I see in Jesus' ministry a more dynamic approach, a comfortability with the essence and ethics of the kingdom that allowed him to engage every person from a different starting point and lead the discussion forward to the kingdom. Jesus customized his persuasion, depending upon the audience. For the rich young ruler, the conversation centered on his attachment to material goods and his self-righteousness about obedience to the Law.[50] Jesus knew how to challenge him in those areas and call for real repentance. Jesus knew how to address the tax collectors and "sinners" as well, for they continually gathered around Jesus, who called for and accepted their repentance.[51] Jesus called Nicodemus to be "born again" (John 3:3). "Born-again" language is common among evangelists and those proclaiming the Word in our day. But I see this phrase on Jesus' lips only once, in conversation with a religious leader, not an unbeliever. "Born again" was a phrase he used nowhere else, suggesting that perhaps this was a challenge custom-suited for Nicodemus and his current life situation. The fluid method of Jesus' proclamation of the kingdom suggests that systematic and programmed approaches to evangelism, while helpful, also must be supplemented with personal knowledge of life in the kingdom.

Failure in evangelism is to be expected. Not everyone will see the point. There are still those who are "worried and upset about many things" distinct from the kingdom (Luke 10:41). There is always a chance that the woman down the street will (and did) sit at my table, graciously allow me to explain the essence of the gospel and the kingdom and tell her what her next steps must be, and then refuse. Our responsibility is not to convert the world. Our responsibility is simply to hold out the message of the kingdom. "It is not our ministry to have the last word. The best we can do is point to Christ and say, 'Hear ye Him.'"[52]

Assessing the Modern Gospel

Finally, while thinking about Jesus' proclamation of the kingdom, we must pause for a moment to think about whether or not our own preaching measures up to that of Jesus. His unwavering message was the arrival of the kingdom and its implementation in the lives of its subjects. His sermon in Nazareth drew upon deliverance themes in Isaiah that speak of mercy and compassion for the oppressed.[53] The Sermon on the Mount (Matt. 5–7) contains counsel on living in compassionate relationship with others (e.g., counsel on anger, lust, divorce, revenge), justice (e.g., "turning the other cheek," giving to the needy, and loving one's enemies), and being right with God (e.g., the right way to pray, fast, and depend upon God for daily provisions). Even when Jesus seemed belligerent toward the Jewish leaders, his cause was usually to either elicit their repentance or to make them think rightly about their acceptance (or rejection) of God's appointed herald, thereby promoting righteousness (their right relationship with God). Jesus' message was intricately bound up with the essence of the kingdom—right standing with God, right living with God's people, and fairness in relationships: mercy, justice, and righteousness.

I got up particularly early one Sunday morning and had some time to kill before church. I sat on the porch and read for an hour or so, came inside, ate breakfast, and then got dressed. There were still twenty minutes before we had to leave for church, so I flipped on the TV. At 9:45 A.M. on a Sunday in the retirement capital of the world, there's nothing but "church" on every channel. One preacher's sermon was titled "Being Comfortable with Your Weight." Another was trying to get me to buy his latest book on prophecy, oil, and Armageddon. This was topped off with an invitation to join another preacher on his Bible cruise in the Bahamas. At the same time, the sources behind *The DaVinci Code* were reviving a centuries-old argument claiming that the four canonical gospels are simply *one* interpretation of Jesus' ministry among a hundred others that (they claim) are also valid.[54] I went to church that morning mentally distant, wondering what Edwards, Whitefield, Spurgeon, Wesley, and Moody would have thought. I kept thinking to myself, "What are we really preaching?"

I am greatly concerned for the state of preaching in the modern church. The synagogue service that Jesus attended (as we have seen) was concerned mostly with the reading of Scripture, not with self-help advice, pop psychology, and topical sermons that don't contain much Scripture for fear of alienating the masses. I can't see Jesus preaching a sermon titled, "The Gospel According to Caesar Augustus," or teaching the crowds "How to Win Friends and Influence Pharisees." After all these centuries, the best preaching is still the proclamation of what God has done in Christ, and that is still the best way to receive and appropriate that good news into everyday living.

Some of you reading this are preachers, and you're on the verge of writing me an e-mail, reminding me that Paul said, "I have become all things to all men so that by all possible means I might save some" (1 Cor. 9:22). Doesn't that imply that there is some level of creativity and art that goes into our preaching, that we can wrap the timeless message of the gospel in new and creative packaging?

Yes, but there was a difference between the evangelistic ministries of Jesus and Paul. Jesus' proclamation was largely to his own compatriots, fellow Jews who had knowledge of the Scriptures. Paul started in the synagogues, as Jesus did, but quickly moved toward evangelistic ministry with the Gentiles. Preaching to the Gentiles caused real challenges for Scripture-loving Paul, for Gentiles did not have knowledge of the Jewish Scriptures. There is evidence that he taught them once they were converted,[55] but if his performance at the Areopagus is any indication of his pattern, Paul sought common ground with Gentiles as a springboard for proclamation of the gospel.

We must heed Marshall McLuhan's warning that "the medium is the message."[56] If all we ever preach are topical sermons, our people will tend to approach the Scriptures topically and may miss the grand narratives of Scripture. If our sermons regularly contain more movie clips and pop-culture images than Scripture, we run the risk of sending the message that while truth is found in Scripture, relevance is found in culture. I am not saying that topical sermons or movie clips are bad. (After all, the subject matter of this book is topical in nature.) I am simply cautioning that it's easy to let the form drive the content. People sometimes remember the forms and forget the message the forms were pointing to. For both Jesus and Paul, whether the message was couched in parable or citations from the pagan poets,[57] those things were never the message themselves. The forms served to enhance the proclamation of the kingdom.

Our proclamation must be centered on the kingdom. That kingdom is one of mercy, justice, and righteousness. It is a kingdom where God reigns supreme and where his people honestly seek to live in genuine harmony with God, one another, and the world around them. This is the kingdom that Jesus was passionate to preach. He did not come to design a privatized, gnostic religion, where salvation is about the acquisition of Bible knowledge. Rather, he came to fashion a community of redeemed people in the new covenant. That work continues today just as it did two millennia ago, and if we are to imitate Jesus' spirituality, we must become people who are passionate about spreading the news of what God continues to do in the world.

So preach the gospel. And by all means, use words.

For Further Reflection

1. What do you think of when you hear the word *preaching*?
2. What was it that Jesus came preaching?
3. How can the kingdom of God be both "near" and "already here" (as the evidence suggests in Jesus' teaching)?
4. How would you respond if someone were to ask you, "What is the kingdom of God?"
5. We have defined the essence of the kingdom as justice, mercy (or compassion), and righteousness. What do you think this means in practical terms?
6. In what ways do you think the church today demonstrates the characteristics of the kingdom?
7. In what areas do you think the church today fails to demonstrate the characteristics of the kingdom?
8. Think of a statement, a parable, or a teaching that Jesus gave during his ministry. Reflect upon how that saying or teaching moves us along toward the essence of the kingdom.

9. Describe a time when you shared the kingdom of God with someone.

10. Describe a time when your offer of the kingdom was rejected.

11. Think of the preaching in the church you attend. Do you think the preaching reflects kingdom values? If so, how? If not, why not?

12. What is the appropriate balance between the eternal truth and creative packaging in modern preaching and worship?

What's Missing?

WE'VE BEEN SEARCHING THE GOSPELS for information related to Jesus' spirituality. We began with the premise that the Gospels contain accurate information about the kinds of practices Jesus routinely engaged in while he was here in the body. We expected that those practices, those "spiritual disciplines," would reveal to us how Jesus fostered, maintained, and allowed the Spirit to grow in his life and ministry. We suspected that Jesus' spirituality was manifested, not in the miraculous healings and exorcisms that he performed in his role as the unique Son of God, but rather in the mundane, everyday practices common to that which is human.

Our quest has not disappointed us. We found that Jesus regularly engaged in honest communication with his Father, fostering the power of God's presence. He was sensitive to the temptations that could have overcome him and cast them down. Jesus was a student of Jewish Scripture and participated in the corporate worship services common to his fellow Jews. He lived a simple life, devoted to doing the will of God; and when opportunities arose for him to assert his own agenda and independence, he reined them in and became submissive to his Father. His spirituality was not isolationist or privatized, though. He shared God's concern for the outcast, the marginalized of society, and he made sure they had a voice in his ministry. He shared fellowship meals with people of all sorts—Pharisees, tax collectors, "sinners," and his own disciples—enacting the great messianic banquet in their presence. And in the midst of all this, the proclamation of the kingdom of God, God's way of living in the world as a redeemed people, was constantly on his lips in preaching and teaching.

These are the practices in which Jesus regularly engaged. They are the daily, routine disciplines that fostered the power of the Spirit in his life. If Jesus is an example of what it means to be spiritual, then we must mimic Jesus' daily life and imitate what we have in common with him, not what is extraordinary and unique to him. Miracles, healings, exorcisms, and walking on water are simply not part of our spirituality. To seek them would probably put us in the category of "a wicked and adulterous generation" asking for a sign (Matt. 12:39; 16:4; cf. Luke 11:29). The miracles were unique to Jesus as the Son of God, as Messiah. We are much more interested in Jesus as our brother, our fellow human, the one who "shared in their humanity" and was "made like his brothers in every way" (Heb. 2:14, 17), and the kind of spirituality that he practiced while in the flesh. If we are to take him as our example, we must begin by giving serious consideration to the disciplines in which he regularly engaged.

But our study is not quite complete. We must now consider what is missing. What is missing from Jesus' routine practice of spirituality that, quite frankly, we expected to be there? What practices that we deem so important to Christian spirituality are strangely absent from the Gospel record in regard to Jesus? This discussion is simultaneously a caution to our study and a critique of modern notions of Christian spirituality. The answers may surprise you.

Fasting

There is surprisingly little record of Jesus fasting in the Gospels. The only time we have explicit mention of Jesus fasting is during the wilderness temptation.[1] Jesus taught his disciples how to fast (Matt. 6:16–18), which presupposes that he knew something about it. Banks suggests that Jesus abstained from food at various times throughout the Gospels, for instance, that Jesus went without food when he got up early to pray and when he was too busy to come away from the crowds and get something to eat.[2] But this is not convincing evidence that Jesus was fasting. Mark 1:35 mentions nothing about fasting in his description of Jesus' morning prayer. Peter's objection, when he found Jesus, was not, "You ought to come get something to eat." Rather, his objection was, "Everyone is looking for you!" (Mark 1:37). When challenged by his family that he considered ministering to the crowds more important than grabbing a bite, his response was not, "I can't eat. I'm fasting" (Mark 3:20–21). Just because he was busy and concerned does not mean he was undertaking the spiritual discipline of fasting.

Once his ministry began, fasting wasn't prominent in Jesus' spiritual regimen. The wilderness temptation was a test preceding his ministry, and once he had passed that test, the Gospels record no fasting on his part. In fact, the accusation leveled against him suggests quite the opposite. Jesus came "eating and drinking" and was called "a glutton and a drunkard" for it (Matt. 11:19; Luke 7:34), suggesting that his practice with regard to food and drink was anything but ascetic. The disciples of John the Baptist questioned him about this, wondering why Jesus' disciples *didn't* fast when they and the Pharisees made a regular habit of it. Jesus' response evoked the imagery of a wedding banquet. No one goes to a wedding reception, where there is food galore in festive celebration, and says, "No thanks. I'm fasting today." To ignore the sumptuous feast provided by the host would be an insult. Jesus likened his ministry to a wedding banquet (with him as the groom) and said that while the wedding party is taking place, fasting is inappropriate. Jesus hinted at the time when he, the bridegroom, would be taken away, and then his disciples would fast.[3] The evidence suggests that *during* his ministry Jesus did not make fasting part of his discipline of spirituality.

Tithing

It certainly raises red flags to suggest that Jesus didn't regularly practice tithing. Those of you in local church ministry will likely object to the mere suggestion that tithing wasn't a part of Jesus' spirituality. We place so much emphasis upon the tithe as a part of mature Christian spirituality that to suggest Jesus' lack of emphasis upon it seems irreverent and irresponsible. After all, if the populace finds out that Jesus didn't place much stock in tithing, then the financial stability of the local church will be in great peril (something I suspect, in light of his twice upturning the temple market, Jesus just might be OK with).

The evidence for Jesus tithing as a regular practice simply isn't there. To be fair, Peter was questioned by the temple officials, "Doesn't your teacher pay the temple tax?" (Matt. 17:24–27). Peter's response was, "Yes, he does." Whether this temple tax (given for administration of worship in the temple) was the same as a tithe (also given for administration of worship) is a matter of debate. Peter indicates that Jesus was faithful in paying it. But this exchange concludes with two statements that cast another light on the question. First, Jesus suggested that because the sons of kings were exempt, he too, as the Son of the King, was exempt from the tax. Second, he agreed to pay the tax (so as not to give his critics any leverage) but then miraculously manifested the levy for Peter and himself out of the mouth of a fish. He did not have the money on hand to pay it (and thus probably had not planned to do so).

Tithing was a complicated thing in ancient Israel. Tithing was required for the firstfruits of the crops, new wine, oil,
sheep's wool, and the firstborn of the flocks.[4] The third year the
tithes were to be shared with the Levites, aliens, orphans, and
widows living among them (Deut. 14:28-29; 26:12). The average
first-century Jew was under pressure from the Pharisees to tithe
beyond that ("mint, dill and cumin"). Jesus believed that "justice,
mercy and faithfulness" (Matt. 23:23) must underlie the practice
of tithing. Spencer and Spencer suggest that the tithing system
in first-century Israel—complete with regulations about whether
to tithe the fruit from your neighbor's tree that hangs over your
fence—was so complicated that it prevented the average person
from tithing accurately.[5] Jesus' counsel was not to forsake the
practice altogether but rather to practice tithing in accordance
with the reason for which it was instituted: to provide sustenance
for those who did not have the means to provide for themselves.
While he was certainly a generous individual, there's simply no
evidence in the Gospels that Jesus practiced tithing, as we would
call for it in the modern church.

Journaling

In some circles today it's a sign of maturity to keep a spiritual journal. A spiritual journal is quite different from a diary.
A diary is a record of the day's events. A spiritual journal is a
record of prayers and a documentation of one's spiritual journey.
My wife has kept a journal since she was a young girl and taught
me almost everything I know about journaling. Our children are
required to keep a journal, writing their thoughts, prayers, and
sermon notes as a record of their growing "in favor with God"
(Luke 2:52). When I teach classes on prayer, in the local church
and at the collegiate level, one of the first things I do is introduce
students to the concept of a prayer journal. "Journaling helps us

examine ourselves systematically"[6] and can be a very effective spiritual discipline.

The practice of recording prayers and musings about godly things is quite ancient. Many of the psalms are David's printed prayers. The proverbs are largely Solomon's musings about spiritual matters. The Evangelists recorded several of Jesus' prayers[7] and a few by the early church.[8] Throughout church history the spiritual journals and autobiographies of men like Augustine, Thomas à Kempis, François Fénelon, Dag Hammerskjöld, Thomas Merton, and Henri Nouwen have brought encouragement to many.

One of the remarkable facts about Christian history is that Jesus never wrote anything for his disciples to pass on. The statement may seem pejorative, and perhaps you're thinking, "Maybe you should say that we have no *record* of Jesus ever writing anything." Surely, with the attention and veneration given to Jesus so quickly after his death, anything he had written would have been copied by his disciples for immediate distribution. Yet, we find nothing, which strongly suggests that Jesus never wrote anything for public consumption. Even if John's account of the woman caught in adultery belongs to the original gospel, John didn't find it worthwhile to record for us what Jesus was writing in the dirt (John 8:6, 8). Self-examination was certainly an aspect of Jesus' spirituality, but he chose not to commit it to print. Of course, with writing materials—papyrus and parchment—being expensive and in short supply, one might well argue that the poor carpenter from Nazareth couldn't have afforded to write much if he wanted to!

Singing

Every church I've ever attended has placed great emphasis upon singing in the corporate worship service. We tend to call it "worship," ignoring the biblical evidence that worship is as much about allegiance to God as it is singing praises to him. Usually about half of the corporate worship service is devoted to singing in some form or another, with the rest of the time given to preaching, the sacraments, and miscellaneous announcements and testimonies.

The Gospels don't record much of Jesus' habits in regard to singing. He attended the synagogue service faithfully, and there may have been some singing there. But we noted earlier that singing wasn't the main focus of the synagogue service. If singing was involved, it took a backseat to prayer and the reading of Scripture. Festive music was part of the temple ceremonies, particularly during the feasts, and Jesus may have participated in some singing as one of the congregants there. However, the Evangelists are silent about it, suggesting that it wasn't important enough for them to record. The only time we find Jesus explicitly singing was in the upper room, at the end of the Passover meal, and Matthew is the only one who mentions it. After Jesus shared the bread and wine with his disciples, they sang a hymn and then went to the Mount of Olives (Matt. 26:30). The song they sang was probably Psalm 114 (or 115), traditionally sung at the end of the Passover liturgy after the distribution of the third cup of wine.[9] This one text is the only explicit evidence we have of Jesus' musical activity.

Beyond this, there is some circumstantial evidence. The author of Hebrews points in Jesus' direction as he quotes Psalm 22:22: "I will sing your praises" (Heb. 2:12). Spencer and Spencer point to this as possible evidence that Jesus made singing a regular part of his spirituality.[10] But rather than making a point about Jesus' singing habits, the author of Hebrews is focused upon the humanity Jesus shared with us, thereby qualifying him for the work of redemption. Jesus and human beings are "of the same family," he argues (Heb. 2:11). The quote from Psalm 22:22 is invoked with emphasis upon this aspect: "I will declare your name to *my brothers*; in the presence *of the congregation* I will sing your praises" (emphasis added). From the cross Jesus also cites lines from two psalms that were set to music, as the notations before each psalm indicate.[11] Jesus' recitation of them from the cross may not have been musical or comprehensive. At best the evidence for any extended practice of singing in the Gospels is minimal.

Repentance

The final thing we find missing from Jesus' spirituality is the practice of repentance and confession. Jesus preached the kingdom's arrival in accordance with repentance,[12] and his parables often called for repentance on the part of his hearers.[13] If we believe that the testimony of Scripture is accurate that Jesus lived a sinless life,[14] then it's blatantly obvious why this never became a practice in Jesus' life. There was nothing in his life from which to repent. Our experience is littered with the dogma of fallen humanity. "To err is human," we say, or, "I'm only human." It's hard to conceive of a spirituality apart from repentance of the things that so egregiously display our sinful condition. Jesus "had to be made like his brothers in every way, in order that he might become a merciful and faithful high priest" (Heb. 2:17), yet the atonement of humanity's sins necessitated a sinless life (Heb. 4:15–5:3). Absolute holiness afforded Jesus the right to atone for the sins of the world, and his sinless life makes moot the necessity of any discipline of repentance in his spirituality. You and I have plenty to repent from, so in this matter Jesus' spirituality is *not* to be imitated.

One Last Caution

Now that we have articulated a number of practices that we *expected* to find more prominent in Jesus' spirituality, we need to leave off with one final caution. We began this study with a few cautionary pieces of advice to guide our study, and so we must end with another warning related to the things just mentioned, those things seemingly absent from Jesus' spirituality.

When I was a graduate student at Cincinnati Bible Seminary,
I had the privilege of studying for a short time with W. W. Winter,
professor of Old Testament. He was a stately gentleman who was
extremely competent in his field. I took two classes with him in
the span of a year. In our many discussions of Old Testament history, we regularly encountered liberal theories that undermined
the historicity of the biblical text, usually on the grounds that
hard evidence was lacking outside the text itself. His response in
those situations serves as a gentle caution for our discussion of
the practices seemingly absent from the Gospels: "Absence of evidence is not always evidence of absence."

He was absolutely right. Just because critics dismissed the historicity of the Old Testament because there was no evidence of the
Hittite empire didn't mean that the Hittites never existed. Archae-
ologists later unearthed the remains of that empire, proving that the
evidence had been there all along, just not where anyone could see it.

The same could be said about the spirituality of Jesus. Just
because fasting isn't prominent in his ministry doesn't mean that
he never fasted. I would argue that he had some proficiency at
it before his forty-day fast in the wilderness, and that when he
taught about it, he spoke from experience. He may have sung more
than the Gospels suggest (per their limitations on musical score in
print). He may have tithed more regularly than they record, and
he may have written some things down. The Evangelists weren't
concerned to pass those things along to us about Jesus' life. Those
weren't the things that were most important to them, and they
didn't feel the need to pass them along to their followers. Our
quest was only to consider, from the evidence available to us, the
things that Jesus did *regularly* or *routinely* that could help us understand what it means to foster the full power of the Holy Spirit.

We must again be cautious regarding journaling and repentance.
I think that on those two fronts we are safe to say that "absence

of evidence *strongly suggests* evidence of absence." Here there are circumstantial factors weighing in from all sides to support our claims.
Theologically the practice of repentance is ludicrous for a sinless
man. Historically, there's absolutely no evidence that Jesus ever had
need or occasion to repent. As for journaling, the weight of literature
and history suggests that had Jesus written anything we certainly
would have found copies of it circulating very soon after his death.

Neither does it follow that absence of any discipline in Jesus'
life warrants excising it from our own. While Jesus didn't practice
repentance, my life and spirituality (and my marriage) would suffer
if I didn't repent of the things that I do wrong. Jesus doesn't seem
to have fasted during his own ministry, but he declared that the
time would come when his disciples *would* fast.[15] So we must be
careful not to claim that just because it wasn't prevalent in Jesus'
life it shouldn't be important to his people. While there were certain aspects of his spirituality that we can never duplicate because
he was the unique Son of God, so also there are certain aspects of
Christian spirituality that must appear in our lives because we are
human, not divine, and subject to frailty. Exactly what those are is
a discussion for another book.

Spiritual, Like Jesus: Well-Rounded Spirituality

If we desire to imitate the spirituality of Jesus, we must take into
account that his spirituality was well-rounded. Most of us tend to
focus on one or two aspects of Christian spirituality and hone our
attention and proficiency in those areas. "Left to ourselves in the
development of our spiritual practices, we will generally gravitate
to those spiritual activities that nurture our preferred pattern of
being and doing."[16] Robert Mulholland argues that eventually the
shadow side—that part of the personality that is being neglected by
our proficiency in other areas—will demand attention. If it doesn't
receive it, it could manifest itself in some ugly ways.[17]

I spent a little over seven years serving as minister of education and worship at a mid-sized church in metropolitan Detroit. When the congregation began to grow, we knew that a systematic plan for discipleship was in order. After two years of planning, discussion, revision, and study on the part of both the staff and the elders, we chose to focus our discipling efforts in six key areas: fellowship, Bible study, service, evangelism, worship, and prayer. We knew that few people would remember them if we didn't communicate it well enough, so we finally settled on the image of an engine block (appropriate for the Detroit area). Each of the core values was represented as a piston in a six-cylinder engine. We continually hammered home that each of the pistons had to be firing *together* for the engine to run properly.

Christian spirituality is no different. If Bible study and prayer are my primary disciplines, I'll be very proficient at the spirituality of introversion. It becomes natural then to forsake the kinds of spiritual disciplines that involve other people—corporate worship, caring for the oppressed, and proclamation. Likewise, if my spirituality is primarily focused on activities involving others, I run the risk of letting other people dictate my spiritual journey on their agenda or of neglecting to deal with what's really going on in my own soul. Christian spirituality in its best expression is well-rounded and holistic.

Jesus demonstrated this kind of holistic spirituality. He spent time caring for his own relationship with the Father. Prayer, casting down temptation, and a conscious submission to his Father ensured that, having saved others, he had not disqualified himself from the prize (as Paul says of himself in 1 Cor. 9:27). But his spirituality wasn't privatized. He spent time in corporate worship with God's redeemed people and offered his table to anyone who would eat with him. He spent time with all kinds of people and was not discriminatory about who he allowed to follow him. He also kept his own priorities front and center, marginalizing the self-motivated and aberrant requests of others by living a simplified life. He got the Word into his own life through his study of Scripture and into the lives of others through his proclamation of the gospel.

It's easy to become one-sided. We gravitate to the things that come easy to us, the things that we enjoy and from which we receive the most inspiration and benefit. Strikingly, Jesus' spirituality wasn't one-sided. He simultaneously gave attention to the various strands of Spirit-living that we have been discussing. Imitating Jesus requires giving attention to the things he gave attention to, caring about the things he cared about, and doing them the way he did them to the best of our ability. Becoming holistic, well-rounded, mature disciples of Jesus requires imitating him in his own spirituality. Let us imitate him in these disciplines and likewise become, as Jesus was, spiritual.

For Further Reflection

1. Why do you think the Gospels say little about Jesus' practice of fasting? Does that mean that he didn't fast?
2. Thinking back through the chapter on fellowship meals and the section in this chapter on fasting, how would you describe Jesus' relationship with food?
3. Does it make you uncomfortable to read that the Gospels are silent about Jesus' tithing? If so, why?
4. Describe some ways in which Jesus was a generous human being.
5. Tithing is surprisingly absent from the portraits of Jesus' life. What does that mean for you and me? Does that mean that we aren't to tithe? What is the Bible's position on tithing?
6. Have you ever kept a spiritual journal? If so, describe the benefit that it has had for your spirituality.

7. Did you ever consider Jesus to be a "singer"? If so, why do you think the Gospels are quiet about his singing?

8. We have no record that Jesus ever repented. Why not? What Scripture verses can you point out to justify your answer?

9. "Absence of evidence is not always evidence of absence." What does that mean? How does it relate to the discussion about fasting, tithing, singing, journaling, and repentance?

10. Our spirituality needs to be well-rounded, not focused solely on one area of our temperament. What is your dominant mode of spirituality? What lies in the "shadow side" of your personality and temperament? (For example, if I am an introvert, then extroversion lies in my shadow side.) How can you engage the shadow side of your spirituality? What benefit do you think it might have?

11. Now that you've considered Jesus' spirituality, in what ways does your practice of faith need adjustment? What qualities do you see in Jesus that are lacking in your own life and need improvement?

Notes

∎

Introduction: What Is "Spiritual"?

1. Stephen C. Barton, *The Spirituality of the Gospels* (Peabody, MA: Hendrickson, 1992), 63.
2. Cheslyn Jones, Geoffrey Wainwright, and Edward Yarnold, eds., *The Study of Spirituality* (Oxford: Oxford University Press, 1986), 58-89.
3. Albert Schweitzer, *The Quest of the Historical Jesus*, trans. W. Montgomery (New York: Macmillan, 1948), 398.
4. John 4:34.
5. Luke 4:18-21; cf. Isa. 61:1-2.
6. *Inf. Gos. Thom.* 14:1-2; 15:1-4.
7. Mark 14:12; Luke 2:41; John 2:23; 5:1; 7:1-13; 10:22-23.
8. Matt. 4:1-2; John 6:14-15.
9. Luke 6:12-16.
10. Matt. 26:36-44; Mark 14:32-40; Luke 22:39-46.
11. Luke 11:37-52; 15:3-16:31; 19:5-10.
12. Walter J. Hollenweger, "Pentecostals and the Charismatic Movement," in *The Study of Spirituality*, ed. Cheslyn Jones, Geoffrey Wainwright, and Edward Yarnold (Oxford: Oxford University Press, 1986), 551-52. For a courteous view of spirituality in the charismatic tradition, see Richard J. Foster, *Streams of Living Water: Celebrating the Great Traditions of Christian Faith* (San Francisco: HarperCollins, 1998), 97-133.
13. Ignatius, *To the Ephesians* 5; Ignatius, *To the Magnesians* 6, 13; Ignatius, *To the Trallians* 13; and Ignatius, *To the Philadelphians* 3.1-3.
14. François Fénelon, *The Seeking Heart* (Jacksonville: The SeedSowers, 1992), 127.

15. Eugene H. Peterson, *The Wisdom of Each Other* (Grand Rapids: Zondervan, 1998), 52.
16. "The Christian life is mostly what is being done to you, not what you are doing." Ibid., 32.
17. John R. Tyson, *Invitation to Christian Spirituality* (Oxford: Oxford University Press, 1999), 46.
18. Thomas à Kempis, *The Imitation of Christ*, trans. Leo Sherley-Price (New York: Penguin, 1952) 1.1.
19. Col. 1:16; John 1:3, 10.
20. Morton Smith, *Jesus the Magician* (San Francisco: Harper and Row, 1978), 35.
21. Matt. 3:16; Mark 1:10; Luke 3:22.
22. Col. 1:15; Phil. 2:6.
23. Matt. 4:1–10; John 6:14–15.
24. Matt. 3:16–17; Mark 1:9–11; Luke 3:21–22.
25. Robert H. Stein, *The Method and Message of Jesus' Teaching* (Philadelphia: Westminster Press, 1978), 80. Jesus addresses God as "Father" sixty-five times in the Synoptics.
26. John 14:15–16, 25–27; 15:26; 16:5–15.

Chapter 1: Prayer and Solitude

1. Karl Barth, *Prayer*, trans. Sara F. Terrien, 2nd ed. (Philadelphia: Westminster Press, 1985), 31.
2. Matt. 13:36.
3. John 2:24.
4. Malcolm Goldsmith, *Knowing Me, Knowing God: Exploring Your Spirituality with Myers-Briggs* (Nashville: Abingdon, 1997), 99–100.
5. Matt. 6:5–6.
6. Mark 1:21–37; Luke 4:40–42.
7. Matt. 14:23–25; Mark 6:45–48; John 6:16–19.
8. J. D. G. Dunn, "Prayer," in *Dictionary of Jesus and the Gospels*, ed. J. B. Green and S. McKnight (Downers Grove, IL: InterVarsity Press, 1992), 617. Dunn suggests that by Jesus' day the tradition may have increased to three times daily.
9. Matt. 14:19; 15:36; Mark 6:41; 8:6–7; Luke 9:16; 24:30; John 6:11, 23.
10. Matt. 11:25–26.

11. For a simple description of the Passover liturgy, see Craig L. Blomberg, *Jesus and the Gospels: An Introduction and Survey* (Nashville: Broadman and Holman, 1997), 331, and the literature cited there.
12. Luke 11:1–4.
13. Matt. 6:9–13; Luke 11:2–4.
14. Matt. 6:7.
15. William David Spencer and Aida Besançon Spencer, *The Prayer Life of Jesus: Shout of Agony, Revelation of Love, a Commentary* (Lanham, MD: University Press of America, 1990), 34.
16. Luke 18:1–8 and Luke 11:5–8, respectively.
17. Matt. 14:19; 15:36; Mark 6:41; 8:6–7; Luke 9:16; John 6:11, 23.
18. Matt. 26:26–27; Mark 14:22–23; Luke 22:17, 19; John 17.
19. Richard J. Foster, *Prayer: Finding the Heart's True Home* (San Francisco: HarperCollins, 1992), 7–15.
20. Luke 22:31–32.
21. See Gen. 48:14.
22. Matt. 19:13–14; Mark 10:13–16; Luke 18:15–17.
23. Luke 21:37.
24. He may have actually encouraged them to "pray standing" (Luke 22:46), as the same vocabulary (*anistēmi*, "stand up") is used to describe Jesus rising from his kneeling position (22:45). Having warned them to be alert in prayer and then finding them asleep, he may have intended them to "pray standing" as a simple means of staying awake and alert.
25. Luke 22:44. However, this verse is disputed in the earliest manuscripts, and scholars are still unsure about what Luke really meant by this.
26. Matt. 26:39, 42; Mark 14:36; Luke 22:42.
27. Isaiah 52:13–53:12.
28. Matt. 3:17; cf. Isa. 42:1; Luke 24:25–27.
29. Matt. 4:8–10; Luke 4:5–8.
30. Origen, *On Prayer* 2.1. In Rowan A. Greer, *Origen: Selected Writings*, The Classics of Western Spirituality (Mahwah, NJ: Paulist Press, 1979), 82.

Chapter 2: Casting Down Temptation
1. Matt. 4:2; Luke 4:2.
2. G. H. Twelftree, "Temptation," in *Dictionary of Jesus and the Gospels*,

ed. J. B. Green and S. McKnight (Downers Grove, IL: InterVarsity Press, 1992), 821-27.

3. John 6:6.

4. Matt. 19:3; 22:18; Mark 10:2; 12:15.

5. One of the later manuscripts of this text suggests that Jesus was writing the sins of her accusers. More likely is the suggestion that, because this was a debate about punishments laid down in the Law, he was writing the legal text forming the basis of his forthcoming verdict.

6. For a brief analysis of the evidence, see Craig L. Blomberg, *The Historical Reliability of John's Gospel* (Downers Grove, IL: InterVarsity Press, 2001), 140; and F. F. Bruce, *The Gospel of John* (Grand Rapids: Eerdmans, 1983), 413-18.

7. Matt. 4:1; Luke 4:1.

8. I am following Matthew's account here (4:1-11). Luke's order is inverted, and I have no intention of engaging the discussion about the reason for the variegation. For a brief discussion, see G. H. Twelftree, "Temptation," 823.

9. C. S. Lewis, *The Lion, the Witch, and the Wardrobe* (1950; reprint, New York: Collier Books, 1970), 159.

10. Gen. 1:1; Exod. 9:29; Job 41:11; Pss. 24:1; 89:11; 95:4-5; 97:1-6; Isa. 6:3; Dan. 6:26; 7:26-27.

11. Isa. 42-56.

12. The combination of verbs describing the Servant as "lifted up and highly exalted" is unique, appearing only four times in the Old Testament, all in Isaiah (6:1; 33:16; 52:13; 57:15) and all in reference to God. See John N. Oswalt, *Isaiah Chapters 40-66* (Grand Rapids: Eerdmans, 1998), 378.

13. See Morna Hooker, *The Son of Man in Mark* (London: SPCK, 1967), 27-30, 103-47. "If we turn again to Daniel, the answer to *this* question is immediately clear: the Son of man can—and will—suffer when his rightful position and God's authority are denied: this is the situation in Dan. 7, where the 'beasts' have revolted against God and have crushed Israel who, as Son of man, should be ruling the earth with the authority granted by God" (p. 108).

14. Dan. 7:1-8.

15. The word used in both Matthew 4:11 and Mark 1:13 is from the *diakoneō* ("serve") word group, a term whose primary meaning denoted food preparation. See W. Bauer, W. F. Arndt, F. W. Gingrich, and F. W. Danker, "*diakoneō*" and "*diakonia*" in *Greek-English Lexicon of the New Testament and Other Early Christian Literature*, 2nd ed. (Chicago: University of Chicago Press, 1979), 184.

16. Outside the Passion narratives, John shares only the feeding of the five thousand (Matt. 14:15-21; Mark 6:35-44; Luke 9:12-17; John 6:4-13), the subsequent walking on the water (Matt. 14:22-33; Mark 6:45-52; John 6:14-21), Jesus' anointing (Matt. 26:6-13; Mark 14:3-9; John 12:2-11), and the triumphal entry (Matt. 21:1-11, 14-17; Mark 11:1-11; Luke 19:28-44; John 12:12-19) with the Synoptics. John's account of Jesus clearing the temple (2:13-22) is early in his ministry and brings a wholly different result than the event recorded by the Synoptics during the final week (Matt. 21:12-13; Mark 11:15-18; Luke 19:45-48).

17. Matt. 14:22-23; Mark 6:45-46.

18. For a simple discussion of the evidence, see Tim Perry, *Mary for Evangelicals: Toward an Understanding of the Mother of Our Lord* (Downers Grove, IL: InterVarsity Press, 2006), 126-28, and the literature cited there.

19. John 7:1-9.

20. John 2:4.

21. Matt. 12:38-39; Luke 11:16; John 2:18-22; 6:30.

22. Matt. 16:1-12; Mark 8:11-15.

23. Matt. 16:21; Mark 8:31; Luke 9:20-22.

24. Matt. 16:23; Mark 8:33.

25. Luke 4:13.

26. John 18:10-11.

27. John 17:15.

28. Matt. 26:38-44; Mark 14:32-41; Luke 22:42-44.

29. Leon Morris, *Hebrews*, Expositor's Bible Commentary (Grand Rapids: Eerdmans, 1971), 50.

30. George Barna, *Growing True Disciples* (Ventura, CA: Issachar Resources, 2000), 54-60.

Chapter 3: Scripture Reading and Memorization

1. Luke 1:46–55; cf. 1 Sam. 2:1–10.
2. 2 Sam. 7:12–16; Isa. 11:1; Ezek. 34:23–24.
3. Matt. 1:19; cf. Deut. 24:1–2.
4. Joel E. Hoffman, "Jewish Education in Biblical Times: Joshua to 933 B.C.E." *Jewish Bible Quarterly* 25, no. 2 (1997): 114; William Barclay, *Educational Ideals in the Ancient World* (Grand Rapids: Baker, 1959), 14-17; Howard Clark Kee, "Defining the First-Century CE Synagogue: Problems and Progress," *New Testament Studies* 41, no. 4 (1995): 481–93; and Lee I. Levine, "The Nature and Origin of the Palestinian Synagogue Reconsidered," *Journal of Biblical Literature* 115, no. 3 (1996): 429–36.
5. Deut. 6:4–9 (commands); Deut. 4:9 and 6:20–25 (the Law); Exod. 13:8 (festivals).
6. James L. Crenshaw, "Education in Ancient Israel," *Journal of Biblical Literature* 104, no. 4 (1985): 614. Many have noted that the counsel, "Son, heed my discipline" and its assorted variations in Proverbs refer to a father's instruction of his son, not to a teacher's instruction of a student.
7. Tradition asserts that in AD 63 Joshua ben Gamla decreed that every town and village should create a school for children to attend, beginning at age six or seven. It is difficult in retrospect to assume that schools were widespread during Jesus' childhood. See Crenshaw, "Education in Ancient Israel," 612, and the literature cited there.
8. Luke 2:47.
9. R. T. France, *Jesus and the Old Testament* (Downers Grove, IL: InterVarsity Press, 1971), 25–37.
10. Matt. 1:3–16; cf. Ruth 4:18–22; 1 Chron. 3:10–16.
11. Matt. 2:5–6, 17–18; cf. Mic. 5:2; Jer. 31:15, respectively.
12. I realize that most modern scholars of the Gospels would disagree with my decision here, and point to the problem of ignoring the Evangelists' citations of Scripture while relying upon their accurate recording of Jesus' citation of Scripture. I am operating from the presupposition that Jesus' statements are recorded accurately and that the Evangelists were responsible enough to make a distinction between the words of Jesus and their own interpretations of his sayings.

13. Luke 24:25–27, 44–47.
14. Gen. 1; John 20:19–23.
15. Exod. 39:30.
16. Deut. 6:9 and Deut. 24:1, 3, respectively.
17. Ian M. Young, "Israelite Literacy: Interpreting the Evidence, Part 1," *Vetus Testamentum* 48, no. 2 (1998): 239–53; and Young, "Israelite Literacy: Interpreting the Evidence, Part 2," *Vetus Testamentum* 48, no. 3 (1998): 408–22. Young suggests that the documents in the Old Testament are generated by the priestly aristocracy and that the examples given there are naturally limited to the upper class, literate men of society.
18. "It therefore seems likely that the sense of the biblical verb 'to write' (*ktb*) can also bear the sense of 'to have someone write for one.' It follows, hence, that not all who are said in the Bible to write, or at least not all who are commanded to write, are necessarily themselves literate. It should be emphasized, nevertheless, that when people are said to have called a scribe, it does not follow that they did so because they could not read or write." Young, "Israelite Literacy, Part 1," 248–49.
19. Leon Morris, *The Gospel According to John*, New International Commentary on the New Testament (Grand Rapids: Eerdmans, 1971), 888–91; and D. A. Carson, *The Gospel According to John* (Grand Rapids: Eerdmans, 1991), 335–37.
20. Mark 2:25; Luke 6:3; cf. Matt. 12:3; 1 Sam. 21:1–6.
21. Matt. 19:4–5; cf. Gen. 1:27; 2:24.
22. Matt. 21:16.
23. Matt. 21:42; Mark 12:10; cf. Ps. 118:22–23.
24. Mark 12:26; cf. Exod. 3:6–16.
25. Exod. 20:1–17.
26. When tempted to turn stones to bread, his response was "man does not live on bread alone" (Matt. 4:4; Luke 4:4; cf. Deut. 8:3). "Do not put the Lord your God to the test" was his response to the suggestion that he make God send angels to rescue him (Matt. 4:7; Luke 4:12; cf. Deut. 6:16). And when Satan asked him to bow down and worship him in exchange for the allegiance of the world's kingdoms, Jesus responded, "Worship the Lord your God, and serve him only" (Matt. 4:10; Luke 4:8; cf. Deut. 6:13).

27. Isa. 42–56.
28. Timothy Wiarda, "Story-Sensitive Exegesis and Old Testament Allusions in Mark," *Journal of the Evangelical Theological Society* 49, no. 3 (2006): 491. N. T. Wright, *Jesus and the Victory of God* (Minneapolis: Fortress, 1996), 600–601, suggests that during his ministry Jesus meditated on Psalm 22 and others that hinted at God's intervention on behalf of the afflicted.
29. France, *Jesus and the Old Testament*, 15, says, "It is not easy, however, to decide what constitutes an allusion to the Old Testament. There is no rule of thumb by which intentional allusions can be detected, and it is possible to see references to the Old Testament in the most innocent everyday language."
30. The five witnesses are John the Baptist (John 5:33–35), the "works" the Father sent him to do (5:36), the Father (5:37–38), the Scriptures (5:39–40), and Moses, who legally functions as an accuser, but still bears testimony to Jesus (5:45–47).
31. In the Hebrew Bible, 1 and 2 Kings were known as a single book. Only later was it divided into two distinct sections. For a brief discussion, see Gleason L. Archer Jr., *A Survey of Old Testament Introduction* (Chicago: Moody, 1994), 311, 317.
32. C. F. D. Moule, "'The Son of Man': Some of the Facts," *New Testament Studies* 41, no. 2 (1995): 277–79; Wright, *Jesus and the Victory of God*, 360–71; and Morna Hooker, *The Son of Man in Mark* (London: SPCK, 1967), 11–32, 81–198.
33. N. T. Wright, *The New Testament and the People of God* (Minneapolis: Fortress, 1992), 215–43.
34. Deut. 6:7.
35. Luke 2:46–47.
36. Many have assumed that Mary Magdalene is the "sinful woman" who anointed Jesus because John says that the woman was Mary (John 12:3). This is a gross distortion of the facts. Jesus was likely anointed twice, once by a "sinful" woman in Galilee (Luke 7:36–50) and once during the final week in preparation for his ministry (Matt. 26:6–13; Mark 14:3–9; John 12:1–8). Only John mentions the woman's name as "Mary," and the connection with Martha, who, along with her sister Mary, figures prominently in the scene before this, suggests that

this Mary was the sister of Martha and Lazarus. The anointing in Luke takes place at the hands of a "sinful woman" who is otherwise unidentified. Luke knows Mary Magdalene, for he mentions her in the very next section (Luke 8:2) and tells us only that seven demons were cast out from her. Mary Magdalene was not involved in either anointing, nor is she identified as a prostitute in the biblical record.

37. There were three gifts given: gold, incense, and myrrh (Matt. 2:11). The assumption is that one gift was given by each of the magi, thereby denoting three of them. But this is not stated in the text.

38. The KJV and NIV of Luke 2:7 both suggest that "there was no room for them in the inn." Luke probably did not mean "hotel" by the term. The term used here (*katalyma*) has the sense of "guest room" or even "dining room." This is the term Luke used to describe the place where the Last Supper was held (22:11). Luke knew the popular term for "hotel" and used it in the parable of the Good Samaritan (10:34). That he did not use it in the birth narrative suggests that Mary and Joseph were not turned away from a hotel but rather from their own family home where Joseph went to be registered for the census (2:4).

39. The NIV reads, "So the law was put in charge to lead us to Christ" (Gal. 3:24). The term Paul uses is that of a schoolmaster, or a tutor, *paidagōgos*.

Chapter 4: Corporate Worship

1. Matt. 11:25–26.
2. Matt. 14:19; Mark 6:41; Luke 9:16; John 6:11.
3. The *proskyneō* ("worship") word group occurs some twenty-five times in the Gospels, mostly in Matthew.
4. Matt. 2:2, 11; 14:33; and John 9:38, respectively. So also the disciples worshiped him just before his ascension (Matt. 28:17; Luke 24:52). Herod disingenuously claimed that he wanted to worship the child Jesus (Matt. 2:8).
5. Note also that John says some Greeks came to the feast to "worship" (John 12:20).
6. Matt. 8:2; 9:18; 20:20; and 15:25, respectively. This use also appears in Jesus' parable of the unmerciful servant, where the servant "fell on his knees" and begged mercy from his master (Matt. 18:26), and in

the account of the women leaving the empty tomb, who, when they saw Jesus, "clasped his feet and worshiped him" (Matt. 28:9). In the parallel accounts of the above-mentioned passages Mark and Luke use other terms for "kneeling," not those normally associated with "worship."

7. The Greek *leitourgia*, or *leitourgeō*, denotes a religious kind of ceremony or service. W. Bauer, W. F. Arndt, F. W. Gingrich, and F. W. Danker, "*leitourgia*," *Greek-English Lexicon of the New Testament and Other Early Christian Literature*, 2nd ed. (Chicago: University of Chicago Press, 1979), 470–71.

8. The Greek *latreia*, or *latreuō*, denotes cultic or religious duties. See ibid., 467.

9. Luke 2:37.

10. Luke 1:74.

11. Matt. 4:10; John 16:2.

12. Roger T. Beckwith, "Daily and Weekly Worship of the Primitive Church in Relation to Its Jewish Antecedents," *Evangelical Quarterly* 56, no. 2 (1984): 70–71.

13. For a detailed discussion of the first-century synagogue service, see Beckwith, "Daily and Weekly Worship," 65–80; Everett Ferguson, *Backgrounds of Early Christianity* (Grand Rapids: Eerdmans, 1987), 456–63; Emil Schürer, *A History of the Jewish People in the Time of Christ*, trans. John MacPherson, 5 vols. (1890; reprint, Peabody, MA: Hendrickson, 1994), 2.2.27; E. Yamauchi, "Synagogue," in *Dictionary of Jesus and the Gospels*, ed. J. B. Green and S. McKnight (Downers Grove, IL: InterVarsity Press, 1992), 781–84; and Hughes Oliphant Old, *The Reading and Preaching of the Scriptures in the Worship of the Christian Church*, 6 vols. (Grand Rapids: Eerdmans, 1998), 1:94–105.

14. Ferguson, *Backgrounds of Early Christianity*, 458.

15. Deut. 6:4–9; 11:13–21; Num. 15:37–41.

16. Ferguson, *Backgrounds of Early Christianity*, 459; Beckwith, "Daily and Weekly Worship," 76–77; and Schürer, *History of the Jewish People*, 2.2.27. All these sources indicate that the fixed form of the Eighteen Benedictions, traditionally spoken during the synagogue service, is found in the late first century. This leaves in question whether the prayers were fixed forms in the synagogue service in Jesus' day.

17. This blessing was to be spoken by a priest, and if none was present, it took the flavor of, "God, bless us with the threefold blessing spoken by Aaron and his sons, the priests." See Ferguson, *Backgrounds of Early Christianity*, 461–62.

18. Instrumental music was an integral part of ceremonial Jewish worship, both in the tabernacle and the temple. Cf. Psalms 68:24–26; 87:7; 1 Chronicles 15:16–22; 2 Chronicles 35:15.

19. See A. Z. Idelsohn, *Jewish Music in Its Historical Development* (New York: Tudor, 1944), 96–97, and the rabbinic literature mentioned there.

20. C. Hassell Bullock, *Encountering the Book of Psalms: A Literary and Theological Introduction* (Grand Rapids: Baker, 2001), 31.

21. Beckwith, "Daily and Weekly Worship," 154–56, suggests that early Christian worship, mimicking that of the first-century synagogue, began the service with the singing of a psalm.

22. Bullock, *Encountering the Book of Psalms*, 26–34, has a fantastic and easily accessible introduction to the musical terms linked with the Psalms.

23. Philo gives much the same description of the synagogue service in every place, noting that the Jews gathered weekly for instruction from the Law, which led to "courage, and temperance, and justice, and piety, and holiness, and every virtue" (*On the Life of Moses* 2:216). Cf. also Philo, *On the Life of Moses* 2:214–16; Philo, *On the Special Laws* 2:61–64ff.; Philo, *That Every Good Person Is Free* 80–83; Philo, *On the Contemplative Life* 30–33; Philo, *Hypothetica* 7:11–13; and Philo, *On the Embassy to Gaius* 156–58. Cf. Josephus, *The Antiquities of the Jews* 16.43–45; 16.164; and Josephus, *Against Apion* 1:208–9; 2:175.

24. Ferguson, *Backgrounds of Early Christianity*, 461.

25. Matt. 4:23; 9:35; 13:54; Mark 1:21, 39; 6:2; Luke 4:15, 44; 13:10.

26. Cf. Acts 13:5, 42; 14:1; 16:13, 16; 17:2, 10, 17; 18:4; 19:8.

27. Mark 1:23–26; Luke 4:33–35.

28. Matt. 12:9–13; Mark 3:1–5; Luke 6:6–10.

29. Luke 13:10–13.

30. For instance, Hanina ben Dosa, who lived in Galilee contemporarily with Jesus. For a brief history on him, see Geza Vermes, *Jesus in His Jewish Context* (Minneapolis: Fortress, 2003), 1–13. On faith healers

and holy men, see G. H. Twelftree, "Demon, Devil, Satan," in *Dictionary of Jesus and the Gospels*, 163–72.

31. John 11:41–44.
32. Matt. 12:11–12; Mark 3:4–5; Luke 6:9–10; 13:15–16.
33. Cf. Jer. 17:21–22; Neh. 13:15–18, both of which prohibit carrying "loads" on the Sabbath.
34. Matt. 12:1–8; Mark 2:23–28; Luke 6:1–5.
35. Matt. 5:23–24.
36. Matt. 6:1–4.
37. Matt. 7:6.
38. Twice, in my opinion, once early (John 2:12–25) and once during the final week (Matt. 21:12–13; Mark 11:15–17; Luke 19:45–46).
39. Heb. 10:25.
40. For instance, Jesus frequently went off alone to spend time in prayer, and in the account of the desert temptation, he prepared for it by spending forty days in solitude. Malcolm Goldsmith, *Knowing Me, Knowing God: Exploring Your Spirituality with Myers-Briggs* (Nashville: Abingdon, 1997), 99–100, lists a number of instances recorded in the Gospels that suggest Jesus had introverted tendencies in his personality.
41. Dietrich Bonhoeffer, *Life Together*, trans. John W. Doberstein (San Francisco: HarperCollins, 1954), 77.
42. I am quite aware that I am greatly simplifying the concepts of the *via negativa* and the *via positiva* for the purposes of this discussion. For a better, but concise description, see Clifton Wolters, ed. and trans., *The Cloud of Unknowing and Other Works* (1961; reprint, New York: Penguin, 1978), 16–17.
43. John 7:37–38.
44. Heb. 9:23–24; 10:1–3.
45. Matt. 23:16–19.
46. Matt. 12:3–4; Mark 2:25–26; Luke 6:3–4.
47. Luke 2:21; cf. Gen. 17:12, Lev. 12:1–5.
48. Luke 2:22–24; cf. Exod. 13:2, 12.
49. Matt. 2:23; Luke 2:39–40.
50. Matt. 4:13; John 2:12.
51. For a brief overview, see M. O. Wise, "Feasts," in *Dictionary of Jesus and the Gospels*, 234–41.

52. Old Testament texts prescribing the feasts include: Passover (Lev. 23:4–8; Num. 28:16–25; Deut. 16:1–8; Ezek. 45:21–24), Tabernacles (Lev. 23:33–43; Num. 29:12–39; Deut. 16:13–17), and Pentecost (Lev. 23:15–22; Num. 28:26–31; Deut. 16:9–12).

53. George W. MacRae, "The Meaning and Evolution of the Feast of Tabernacles," Catholic Biblical Quarterly 22 (1960): 269.

54. Craig L. Blomberg, The Historical Reliability of John's Gospel (Downers Grove, IL: InterVarsity Press, 2001), 140n.190, cites some who think that significant time had elapsed between John 7:52 and 8:12, suggesting that the Feast of Tabernacles is no longer in view after 7:52. Blomberg denies the plausibility of this line of thinking and says that "the continuation of imagery so tightly tied in with Tabernacles suggests otherwise."

55. John 7:53–8:11; 9:1–39; and 7:14–39; 8:12–59; 9:40–10:21, respectively.

56. See Leon Morris, The Gospel According to John, New International Commentary on the New Testament (Grand Rapids: Eerdmans, 1971), 419–47, 435–37; MacRae, "Meaning and Evolution of the Feast of Tabernacles," 269–74.

57. Dan. 9:25–27; Matt. 24:15; Luke 21:20.

58. For more of the historical details surrounding the "abomination of desolation" and the dedication of the temple, see 1 Maccabees 1:15–64; 4:36–61; 2 Maccabees 5:15–6:11; 6:18–31; 10:1–9.

59. Exod. 12.

60. John 2:12–23.

61. John 6:1–15, 25–71.

62. Marjorie Thompson, Family the Forming Center: A Vision of the Role of Family in Spiritual Formation (Nashville: Upper Room Books, 1996), 91–102, suggests several family holiday activities for use during Christmas (or Advent), Easter (or Lent), Halloween, Valentine's Day, and significant spiritual milestones in the life of the individual (such as conversion or confirmation, marriage, and death).

63. Ibid., 87.

Chapter 5: Submission

1. Harold C. Gardiner, ed., introduction to The Imitation of Christ, by Thomas à Kempis, trans. Richard Whitford (New York: Doubleday,

1955), 8–9; and Brother Leo, introduction to *The Imitation of Christ*, by Thomas à Kempis, trans. Brother Leo, F. S. C. (1910; reprint, New York: Macmillan, 1950), xxxii.

2. Ignatius, *To the Ephesians*, 5. This idea of hierarchical unity is prominent in his letters: *To the Magnesians* 6, 13; *To the Trallians*, 13; and *To the Philadelphians*, 3.1–3.

3. *Infancy Gospel of Thomas*, 14–15.

4. Ibid., 3–4.

5. Luke 2:1–5.

6. Luke 2:21–24, 39.

7. John 19:25–27.

8. Rom. 13:1–2.

9. The place of the Mosaic Law in the very fabric of Jewish life is evident in G. F. Moore, *Judaism in the First Centuries of the Christian Era: The Age of the Tannaim*, 2 vols. (Cambridge, MA: Harvard University Press, 1962), 2:180–89.

10. Matt. 8:4; Mark 1:44; Luke 5:14.

11. Matt. 17:24–27; the temple tax was levied against the people to pay for temple upkeep and operations.

12. Matt. 22:15–22; Mark 12:13–17; Luke 20:20–26.

13. Matt. 22:17; Mark 12:14–15; Luke 20:22.

14. Robert H. Stein, *The Method and Message of Jesus' Teaching* (Philadelphia: Westminster Press, 1978), 80.

15. For a brief assessment, see Craig L. Blomberg, *Jesus and the Gospels: An Introduction and Survey* (Nashville: Broadman and Holman, 1997), 164–65.

16. "Eating the flesh" and "drinking the blood" of the Son of Man have little to do with Communion here (though one can see how hindsight could lead us to a symbolic understanding). If the dominant metaphor is "bread," then the way one incorporates bread is to eat it. Jesus is the Bread of Life, and that he uses the metaphor "eating" simply affords well with the imagery of bread. The overall message is about taking Jesus seriously and incorporating his teachings.

17. John 10:11–13; cf. Isa. 56:9–57:10; Jer. 23:1–8; Ezek. 34.

18. Matt. 26:39, 42, 44; Mark 14:36, 39; Luke 22:42.

19. Isa. 51:17–22.

20. Isa. 50:8-9; 53:10-12.
21. Nathan O. Hatch, *The Democratization of American Christianity* (New Haven: Yale University Press, 1989), 17-49.
22. Quoted in James North, *Union in Truth: An Interpretive History of the Restoration Movement* (Cincinnati: Standard, 1994), 14-15.
23. Hatch, *Democratization of American Christianity*, 70.
24. James DeForest Murch, *Christians Only: A History of the Restoration Movement* (Cincinnati: Standard, 1962), 83-85.
25. Alexander Campbell, *The Christian System* (1835; reprint, Nashville: Gospel Advocate, 1970), xii.
26. 1 Sam. 15:1-33.

Chapter 6: Simplicity

1. Richard J. Foster, *Celebration of Discipline: The Path to Spiritual Growth*, 3rd ed. (San Francisco: HarperCollins, 1998), 92.
2. Thomas R. Kelly, *A Testament of Devotion* (1941; reprint, San Francisco: HarperCollins, 1992), 90-91.
3. Henri Nouwen, *The Genesee Diary* (New York: Doubleday, 1981), 14.
4. David Fiensy, "Poverty and Wealth in the Gospels and Acts," in *Faith in Practice: Studies in the Book of Acts*, ed. David A. Fiensy and William D. Howden (Atlanta: European Evangelistic Society, 1995), 300-323; Robert H. Stein, *Luke*, The New American Commentary (Nashville: Broadman, 1992), 49-50; and D. A. Carson, Douglas J. Moo, and Leon Morris, *An Introduction to the New Testament* (Grand Rapids: Zondervan, 1992), 129-31. For a brief overview of the chasm between the rich and the poor in the New Testament, see Stephen J. Friesen, "Injustice or God's Will? Early Christian Explanation of Poverty," in *Wealth and Poverty in Early Church and Society*, ed. Susan R. Holman (Grand Rapids: Baker, 2008), 17-36.
5. Luke 11:3; 12:22, 29; Acts 6:1.
6. Matt. 6:28, 31; Luke 12:27-28.
7. Acts 4:34-37.
8. John 1:35-40.
9. E.g., note the cases of Jairus, who brought the concern of his dying daughter (Matt. 9:18-19; Mark 5:21-24; Luke 8:40-42), the woman from Syrophoenicia, whose daughter lay at home possessed (Matt.

15:21-28; Mark 7:24-30), a royal official, whose son lay dying at Capernaum (John 4:43-54), and the request of Mary and Martha to come and heal their brother Lazarus (John 11:1-3).

10. E.g., the deaf and mute man whose friends brought him to Jesus (Mark 7:31-32), the paralytic whose friends lowered him through the roof (Matt. 9:2; Mark 2:3-5; Luke 5:18-20), the blind man healed at Bethsaida (Mark 8:22-26), the possessed boy brought by his father (Matt. 17:14-21; Mark 9:14-29; Luke 9:37-43), and the children who were brought for blessing (Matt. 19:13; Mark 10:13; Luke 18:15).

11. E.g., the deaf and dumb demoniac (Matt. 12:22-23; Luke 11:14), the blind (Bartimaus and others, Matt. 20:29-34; Mark 10:46-52; Luke 18:35-43), the woman with the issue of blood (Matt. 9:20-22; Mark 5:25-34; Luke 8:43-48), and the ten lepers (Luke 17:11-19). Note also the repeated statements that the sick, the lame, and the oppressed were continually brought to Jesus for healing (Matt. 8:16-17; 15:29-31; Mark 1:32-34; Luke 4:40-41).

12. E.g., disputes about who was the greatest in the kingdom (Matt. 18:1; Mark 9:33-34; Luke 9:46; 22:24), the request of James and John to sit in places of honor in his kingdom (Matt. 20:20-21; Mark 10:35-37), the request for Jesus to settle an inheritance dispute (Luke 12:13), and the request of Martha for Jesus to arbitrate an argument with her sister (Luke 10:38-42).

13. Mark 3:20-21.

14. Matt. 8:18; Mark 1:35-37; 4:36; 9:30; Luke 4:42-43; John 6:15.

15. John 3:1-2; 4:40-41.

16. Or continued. His statements early in his ministry were "the kingdom of God *has come*" (*ōngiken*; Matt. 4:17; Mark 1:4).

17. The Song of the Suffering Servant (Isa. 42-56), very prominent in Jesus' thinking and teaching, suggests that the Servant will die on behalf of Israel and then be vindicated (50:4-9; 52:13-53:12).

18. 1 Tim. 6:17; 2 Tim. 4:10; cf. 2 Cor. 4:4.

19. Rom. 14:17; 1 Cor. 4:20; 6:9-10; 15:50; Gal. 5:21; Eph. 5:5; Col. 1:13; 2 Tim. 4:18.

20. See Matthew 20:15 where the literal translation is "or is your eye evil because I am good?" For the "evil eye" as a reference to greed, see Deuteronomy 15:9; 28:54, 56; Proverbs 23:6; 28:22; and Mark 7:22.

The opposite, a "healthy eye," is an idiom for generosity in Proverbs 22:9; Matthew 6:23 (though see further discussion); and Luke 11:34.

21. The word here is *haplous*. See W. Bauer, W. F. Arndt, F. W. Gingrich, and F. W. Danker, "*haplous*," *Greek-English Lexicon of the New Testament and Other Early Christian Literature*, 2nd ed. (Chicago: University of Chicago Press, 1979), 86. See also D. A. Carson, *Matthew*, Expositor's Bible Commentary, ed. Frank E. Gaebelein (Grand Rapids: Zondervan, 1984), 8:178.

22. Matt. 6:25–34.

23. Luke 9:51–56.

24. I. H. Marshall, *The Gospel of Luke*, New International Greek Testament Commentary (Grand Rapids: Eerdmans, 1978), 409–10; and John Nolland, *The Gospel of Matthew*, New International Greek Testament Commentary (Grand Rapids: Eerdmans, 2005), 365–67.

25. "The urgency of the task of preaching the gospel could not be clearer." Marshall, *Gospel of Luke*, 412.

26. Cf. Deuteronomy 21:15–17, which suggests that the older brother (or more specifically, the firstborn of two wives) is to receive a double portion of the inheritance. Families sometimes agreed to keep the farm or estate intact, rather than divide it up and sell it, in order to maintain the profitability of the estate. See Darrell L. Bock, *Luke*, ed. Grant R. Osborne, The IVP New Testament Commentary Series (Downers Grove, IL: InterVarsity Press, 1994), 224.

27. David Wenham, *The Parables of Jesus* (Downers Grove, IL: InterVarsity Press, 1989), 106, suggests that in the parable of the prodigal son, the older son received two-thirds of the estate, while the younger son received a third. B. B. Scott, *Hear Then the Parable* (Minneapolis: Fortress, 1989), 109, cautions, "Whether this conforms to normal Jewish family practice is debated."

28. The words certainly imply that he was out of his mind (*elegon gar hoti exestē*, "for they were saying that he is out of it"), a frequent result of demon-possession in the Gospels.

29. "Take charge" is *krateō*, meaning "to arrest" and implies a taking by force. See Bauer, Arndt, Gingrich, and Danker, "*krateō*," *Greek-English Lexicon*, 448.

30. Mark 3:20–35.

31. John 7:6-8.
32. Luke 10:38-42.
33. Given that this account in Luke falls immediately upon the heels of the parable of the Good Samaritan, the emphasis Luke presents for us may be on the difference between that which is *urgent* (priests and Levites performing their ministries in the temple [10:31-32]; Martha making her preparations [10:40]) and that which is *important* (taking care of the wounded [10:33-35]; listening to Jesus' teaching [10:39]).
34. Mark 10:32-34, 45.
35. Matt. 20:20-23; Mark 10:35-39; cf. Isa. 51:17-23.
36. Luke 21:37; cf. John 8:1.
37. Matt. 26:6-13; Mark 14:3-9; John 12:1-8.
38. Roberta C. Bondi, *To Love as God Loves: Conversations with the Early Church* (Philadelphia: Fortress, 1987), 67-70, reminds us that they also went to the desert to fight the demons.
39. François Fénelon, *The Seeking Heart* (Jacksonville: The SeedSowers, 1992), 127.
40. Matt. 10:37-38; Mark 8:34-35; Luke 14:25-27.
41. E.g., the rich young ruler, Matt. 19:21; Mark 10:21; Luke 18:22.
42. Foster, *Celebration of Discipline*, 85.

Chapter 7: Care for the Oppressed

1. For anonymity's sake, this is neither his name nor the name of the high school.
2. T. E. Schmidt, "Taxes," in *Dictionary of Jesus and the Gospels*, ed. J. B. Green and S. McKnight (Downers Grove, IL: InterVarsity Press, 1992), 805-6.
3. For more on the social status of tax collectors, see Joachim Jeremias, *Jerusalem in the Time of Jesus* (Philadelphia: Fortress, 1969), 310-12.
4. Matt. 9:10-11; Mark 2:15-16; Luke 5:29-30.
5. Matt. 9:11; Mark 2:16; Luke 5:30; 7:36-39; 15:1-2.
6. M. J. Wilkins, "Sinner," in *Dictionary of Jesus and the Gospels*, 758-59.
7. E. P. Sanders, *Jesus and Judaism* (Philadelphia: Fortress, 1985), 177-88; and K. Rengstorf, "*hamartō los, anamartētos*," *Theological Dictionary of the New Testament*, ed. G. Kittel and G. Friedrich, trans. G. W. Bromiley, 10 vols. (Grand Rapids: Eerdmans, 1964), 1:327.

8. Scot McKnight, A *Light Among the Gentiles: Jewish Missionary Activity in the Second Temple Period* (Minneapolis: Fortress, 1991), 12–25.
9. In the Sermon on the Mount (Matt. 5:46–47) Jesus' argument is simply that loving those who return that love is universal; loving *enemies* is Israel's call to live out Yahweh's kingdom. Church discipline is in view in Matthew 18:17, and Jesus' counsel centers around those who continually refuse the counsel of the church. They are to be treated like "outsiders," and to most in his hearing "pagans and tax collectors" were certainly not part of the "in" crowd.
10. Matt. 8:5–13; Luke 7:1–10.
11. Luke 17:11–14; John 4:1–42.
12. Matt. 15:21–28; Mark 7:24–30.
13. Stephen J. Friesen, "Satan's Throne, Imperial Cults, and the Social Settings of Revelation," *Journal for the Study of the New Testament* 27, no. 3 (2005): 370–71, suggests that not more than 3 percent of those in urban settings were rich, with another 5–8 percent living just above the subsistence level. This leaves, in his estimation, 89 percent of the populace living below the level of daily subsistence. With minor variations in various locations, this seems an adequate description of life throughout the Roman Empire, including Judea.
14. John 18:15.
15. Cf. Luke 12:16–21; 14:12–14; 16:13–15; 18:18–27.
16. Matt. 9:20–22; 8:1–4; 9:27–31; and 20:29–34, respectively.
17. Matt. 14:13–21; 15:32–39.
18. Matt. 11:1–5; Luke 7:22.
19. Matt. 19:21; Mark 10:21; Luke 18:22.
20. Luke 11:41; 14:13.
21. Matt. 26:7; Mark 14:3; John 12:1–3.
22. Howard Thurman, *Jesus and the Disinherited* (Boston: Beacon Press, 1976), 106.

Chapter 8: Fellowship Meals

1. Esther 4:3, 15–16; Isa. 58:1–14; Matt. 6:16–18; 9:15.
2. Deut. 21:20; Prov. 23:2; Phil. 3:19.
3. For an introduction to the variety of terms used to describe the religious feasts of ancient Israel, see C. E. Armerding, "Festivals and

Feasts," *Dictionary of the Old Testament Pentateuch*, ed. T. Desmond Alexander and David W. Baker (Downers Grove, IL: InterVarsity Press, 2003), 301-4.

4. See Ezekiel 29:3-5; 32:2-8; and Psalm 74:13-14. David taunted Goliath that he would feed his flesh to the birds (1 Sam. 17:46). Jezebel's body was given to the wild dogs in God's judgment (2 Kings 9:10, 30-37).

5. S. S. Bartchy, "Table Fellowship," *Dictionary of Jesus and the Gospels*, ed. J. B. Green and S. McKnight (Downers Grove, IL: InterVarsity Press, 1992), 796.

6. *m.Abot* 3:2: "If two sit together and words of the Law [are spoken] between them, the Divine Presence rests between them."

7. See Craig L. Blomberg, *Contagious Holiness: Jesus' Meals with Sinners* (Downers Grove, IL: InterVarsity Press, 2005), 95.

8. C. T. McMahan, *Meals as Type-Scenes in the Gospel of Luke* (Ph.D. diss., Southern Baptist Theological Seminary, 1987), 1; quoted in Blomberg, *Contagious Holiness*, 163.

9. "Entertainment" included singing, dancing, and sometimes sex. Bartchy, "Table Fellowship," 798-99; Blomberg, *Contagious Holiness*, 86-87; and Dennis E. Smith, "Table Fellowship as a Literary Motif in the Gospel of Luke," *Journal of Biblical Literature* 106, no. 4 (1987): 614-17.

10. Blomberg, *Contagious Holiness*, 86-96.

11. Ibid., 52.

12. John 3:1-2; 7:50-52; 19:38-42, respectively.

13. Luke 13:31.

14. The fox was a metaphor for insignificance or something of a nuisance not to be taken too seriously. Tobiah the Ammonite jeered that the rebuilt walls of Jerusalem were so poorly constructed that even a fox would cause them to crumble (Neh. 4:3). Solomon spoke of the nuisance of "the little foxes" that ruin the vineyard (Song 2:15). Jesus' reply was to call Herod a "fox" and remind the Pharisees that his death lay ahead in Jerusalem, not Herod's palace (Luke 13:32-33).

15. Luke 14:15.

16. Matt. 9:11; Mark 2:16; Luke 5:30.

17. See Walter L. Liefeld, *Acts*, Expositor's Bible Commentary, ed. Frank E. Gaebelein (Grand Rapids: Zondervan, 1984), 9:1007.

18. The term *diegonguzon* ("muttering") is imperfect, suggesting continuous action.

19. Through the parable of the Lost Son; Luke 15:28.

20. R. T. France, *The Gospel of Mark*, New International Greek Testament Commentary (Grand Rapids: Eerdmans, 2002), 108.

21. Luke says that she "welcomed" him (*hupodechomai*), a word that elsewhere in Luke denotes table context (cf. Acts 19:6). See I. H. Marshall, *The Gospel of Luke*, New International Greek Testament Commentary (Grand Rapids: Eerdmans, 1978), 450–54; and Darrell L. Bock, *Luke 9:51–24:53* (Grand Rapids: Baker, 1996), 1040–41.

22. Matt. 26:6–13; Mark 14:1–10; John 12:1–10.

23. John 14–16.

24. Matt. 14:13–21; Mark 6:30–44; Luke 9:10–17; John 6:1–15.

25. Matt. 15:29–39; Mark 8:1–10; John 6:1–15.

26. Grimm distinguishes between "staple food," which one needs to survive, and "prestige food," which is brought out on the best occasions. Veronika Grimm, *From Feasting to Fasting: The Evolution of a Sin* (New York: Routledge, 1996), 11–12.

27. The NIV suggests that "Jesus declared all foods 'clean,'" but a more literal translation reads, "It does not go into his heart but into his stomach, and goes out into the latrine, cleansing all food." See Larry Hurtado, *Mark*, New International Biblical Commentary (Peabody, MA: Hendrickson, 1989), 113–14.

28. Ranking guests by their seating arrangements around the tables and providing the more important guests with richer kinds of food was a common convention of first-century table fellowship. See Jerome Neyrey, "Ceremonies," in *The Social World of Luke-Acts: Models for Interpretation*, ed. Jerome Neyrey (Peabody, MA: Hendrickson, 1991), 364–65; and Smith, "Table Fellowship."

29. Neyrey, "Ceremonies," 380.

Chapter 9: Evangelism and Proclamation

1. Robert H. Stein, *The Method and Message of Jesus' Teaching* (Philadelphia: Westminster Press, 1978), 1–32.

2. See W. Bauer, W. F. Arndt, F. W. Gingrich, and F. W. Danker, "kēryx,"Greek-English Lexicon of the New Testament and Other Early Christian Literature, 2nd ed. (Chicago: University of Chicago Press, 1979), 431; and G. Friedrich, "kēryx," Theological Dictionary of the New Testament, ed. G. Kittel and G. Friedrich, trans. G. W. Bromiley, 10 vols. (Grand Rapids: Eerdmans, 1964), 3:683–96.

3. Friedrich, "kēryx," 3:683–96, points out that the noun herald never appears in the New Testament in reference to Jesus. Nevertheless, Jesus demonstrates many of the qualities characteristic of heralds in the first-century world.

4. G. R. Beasley-Murray, Jesus and the Kingdom of God (Grand Rapids: Eerdmans, 1986), 100–103.

5. Stein, Method and Message of Jesus' Teaching, 68–79.

6. M. D. Johnson, The Purpose of the Biblical Genealogies (Cambridge: Cambridge University Press, 1969), 74–82.

7. This is most clear in Matthew's genealogy of Jesus, where Josiah is listed as the father of Jehoiachin, though he was in reality his grandfather (Matt. 1:11; cf. 1 Chron. 3:15–16). Matthew presents Shealtiel as the father of Zerubbabel, when the Chronicler demonstrates that he was literally Zerubbabel's uncle (Matt. 1:12; cf. 1 Chron. 3:17–18). That he was connected to the bloodline was apparently enough to reckon him a descendant.

8. Matt. 13:31–32; 13:3–9; 13:47–50; 20:1–16; and 25:1–13, respectively.

9. Leslie C. Allen, The Books of Joel, Obadiah, Jonah, and Micah, New International Commentary on the Old Testament (Grand Rapids: Eerdmans, 1976), 372–73.

10. Thomas E. McComiskey, Micah, Expositor's Bible Commentary, ed. Frank E. Gaebelein (Grand Rapids: Zondervan, 1985), 7:437.

11. Harris, "ḥesed" in Theological Wordbook of the Old Testament, ed. R. L. Harris, G. L. Archer Jr., and B. K. Waltke, 2 vols. (Chicago: Moody, 1980), 1:698–700.

12. Matt. 5:20.

13. Matt. 5:13–16; Luke 8:16–18.

14. Rom. 3:21–28; 2 Cor. 5:21.

15. Rom. 8:1–12; Eph. 4:17–5:20; Col. 3:1–17; 1 Thess. 4:3–8.

16. Matt. 4:23; Mark 1:21, 39; Luke 4:14–15.

17. When Jesus first arrived in Nazareth, he preached in the synagogue (Matt. 13:54; Mark 6:2; Luke 4:16). On several occasions the Gospels record that his modus operandi was to frequent the synagogues in the various towns and villages (Matt. 9:35; cf. Mark 6:6). On two separate occasions, Luke mentions that Jesus was going through the villages preaching and teaching, presumably both as he traveled and in the synagogues on the Sabbath (Luke 8:1; 13:22).

18. Matt. 12:9-13; Mark 3:1-5; Luke 6:6-10.

19. Luke 13:10-17.

20. Mark 1:21-22; Luke 4:31-32.

21. John 7:16-39.

22. John 8:19-58.

23. E.g., the forgiveness of the woman caught in adultery (John 7:53-8:11) and the healing of the man born blind (John 9:1-7).

24. John 10:22-42.

25. Matt. 21:23; Mark 11:15-18; Luke 19:47; 20:1; 21:37-38.

26. E.g., as he was questioned about his authority (Matt. 21:23-27; Mark 11:27-33; Luke 20:1-8) and in his question about David's son (Matt. 22:41-46; Mark 12:35-37; Luke 20:41-44).

27. Matt. 21:33-46; Mark 12:1-12; Luke 20:9-19.

28. Matt. 13:1-3; Mark 2:13; 4:1-2; Luke 5:1.

29. Mark 2:2; Luke 5:17-18.

30. Matt. 5:1-2.

31. Luke 6:17-18.

32. In several places the Gospels mention that he taught the crowds (sometimes comprised of thousands) without mentioning the exact location: Matthew 15:10; Mark 6:34; Luke 9:11; 12:1; 15:1-2; John 4:40-41; 10:41.

33. Rom. 12:6-8; 1 Cor. 12:4-11; Eph. 4:11-13.

34. The two most notable are A. B. Bruce, *The Training of the Twelve* (1894; reprint, Grand Rapids: Kregel, 1971); and Robert E. Coleman, *The Master Plan of Evangelism* (Old Tappan, NJ: Revell, 1964).

35. Matt. 10:5-8.

36. Matt. 10:9-12; Mark 6:8-10. Mark presents Jesus saying, "Take nothing," but Matthew's text gives us a clearer picture of Jesus' intentions. Matthew's Greek forbids the procurement of *extra* supplies,

forbidding the disciples from spending large chunks of time stocking
up for their journey. The ministry is urgent and worthy of immediate
attention. See W. Bauer, W. F. Arndt, F. W. Gingrich, and F. W.
Danker, "*ktaomai*," *Greek-English Lexicon of the New Testament and Other
Early Christian Literature*, 2nd ed. (Chicago: University of Chicago
Press, 1979), 455.
37. Matt. 10:17–39.
38. Matt. 10:32–33, 40–42.
39. To establish everything by the "testimony of two or three witnesses"
(Deut. 19:15).
40. Hughes Oliphant Old, *The Reading and Preaching of the Scriptures in
the Worship of the Christian Church*, 6 vols. (Grand Rapids: Eerdmans,
1998), 1:142–43, states, "While New Testament scholars will hasten to
assure us that Matthew's Sermon to the Disciples was constructed by
the Evangelist from various sources and hardly represents an actual
sermon that Jesus preached at a particular time and place, there is
nevertheless every reason to believe that it was a typical sermon, a
sermon which in one variation or another Jesus often preached."
41. Joel B. Green and Scot McKnight, eds., *Dictionary of Jesus and the
Gospels* (Downers Grove, IL: InterVarsity Press, 1992), 1–10, 116–17.
42. In the famous passage from the noncanonical *Psalms of Solomon*
(17:26–32), the Messiah cleanses Jerusalem, preparing the way for the
nations to gather from the ends of the earth to marvel at him. See
Scot McKnight, *A Light Among the Gentiles: Jewish Missionary Activity
in the Second Temple Period* (Minneapolis: Fortress, 1991), 50–51; and
Beasley-Murray, *Jesus and the Kingdom of God*, 171.
43. "Lifestyle evangelism" is sometimes described in Peter's words,
placing profound emphasis upon godly living as an attractive quality
that unbelievers will seek from Christians. But Aldrich cautions us
that lifestyle evangelism is never a quiet attraction but a lifestyle from
which an eventual proclamation of the gospel springs. "Persuasion is
impossible without some kind of proclamation. Evangelism involves
both good works and good words"; Joseph C. Aldrich, *Lifestyle Evangelism: Crossing Traditional Boundaries to Reach the Unbelieving World*
(Portland: Multnomah, 1981), 82.
44. Matt. 19:16–22; Mark 10:17–22; Luke 18:18–23.

45. Luke 11:53–54; Mark 12:12.
46. John 6:60–66.
47. Matt. 11:16–17; Luke 7:31–32.
48. Matt. 11:20–24; Luke 10:13–15.
49. Luke 4:28–29.
50. Matt. 19:20–21; Mark 10:20–21; Luke 18:21–22.
51. Matt. 21:31–32; Luke 15:1–2.
52. Old, *Reading and Preaching of the Scriptures*, 1:146.
53. Luke 4:16–19; Isa. 61:1–9.
54. This thesis is popularized in our day by Bart D. Ehrman, *Lost Christianities: The Battles for Scripture and the Faiths We Never Knew* (Oxford: Oxford University Press, 2003).
55. To the Roman congregation Paul quotes a fair amount of Scripture as he outlines the gospel, and to support his arguments he appeals to the accounts of Abraham (Rom. 4:1–3; cf. Gen. 15:1–6) and Adam (Rom. 5:12–19; cf. Gen. 3:1–24) without retelling the stories. We can only infer that the Romans previously knew or had access to the Hebrew Scriptures for the illustrations to be effective. The same could be said for his use of the story of Hagar and Sarah (Gal. 4:21–31; cf. Gen. 16:1–16; 21:8–21) and of Moses leading the Hebrews across the Red Sea and into the desert (1 Cor. 10:1–5). He often quotes from the Old Testament without giving a reference or explanation, suggesting that his readers were familiar with those texts. Some examples include "the two will become one flesh" (Eph. 5:31; cf. Gen. 2:24), "every matter must be established by the testimony of two or three witnesses" (2 Cor. 13:1; cf. Deut. 19:15), "honor your father and mother" (Eph. 6:2–3; cf. Exod. 20:12), and an allusion to passages in Jeremiah and Ezekiel with the phrase "peace and safety" (1 Thess. 5:3; cf. Jer. 6:14; Ezek. 13:10–16).
56. Marshall McLuhan, *Understanding Media: The Extensions of Man*, 2nd ed. (New York: Signet, 1964), 23–35.
57. Paul quotes from pagan sources several times in his writings. "Bad company corrupts good character" (1 Cor. 15:33) appears in Menander's play *Thais*. "For in him we live and move and have our being" (Acts 17:28) is a line taken from a poem in which Minos of Crete addresses Zeus as his father. In the same verse Paul quotes Aratus of

Soli's *Phaenomena*, when he says, "We are his offspring." Paul warns
Titus about the reputation that "Cretans are always liars, evil brutes,
lazy gluttons" in a line taken from a work by Epimenides of Crete
(Titus 1:12).

Conclusion: What's Missing?

1. Matt. 4:2; Luke 4:2.
2. R. Banks, "Fasting," *Dictionary of Jesus and the Gospels*, ed. J. B. Green
   and S. McKnight (Downers Grove, IL: InterVarsity Press, 1992), 234.
3. Matt. 9:14–15; Mark 2:18–20; Luke 5:33–35.
4. Cf. Deut. 12:6–7; 18:4–5.
5. William David Spencer and Aida Besançon Spencer, *The Prayer Life of
   Jesus: Shout of Agony, Revelation of Love, a Commentary* (Lanham, MD:
   University Press of America, 1990), 75.
6. Simon Chan, *Spiritual Theology* (Downers Grove, IL: InterVarsity
   Press, 1998), 156. For a simple introduction to the spiritual journal,
   see Ron Klug, *How to Keep a Spiritual Journal* (Minneapolis: Augsburg,
   2002).
7. E.g., as he teaches his disciples to pray (Matt. 6:9–13; Luke 11:2–4), as
   a preface to the raising of Lazarus (John 11:41–42), what scholars call
   his "High Priestly Prayer" in the upper room (John 17), his prayer of
   agony in the garden (Matt. 26:36–44; Mark 14:32–39; Luke 22:41–44),
   and one spontaneously offered thanking God for revealing kingdom
   wisdom to the disciples (Matt. 11:25–26).
8. Over the choosing of Judas's replacement (Acts 1:24–25) and for
   courage in the face of persecution (Acts 4:24–30).
9. Craig L. Blomberg, *Jesus and the Gospels: An Introduction and Survey*
   (Nashville: Broadman and Holman, 1997), 331.
10. Spencer and Spencer, *Prayer Life of Jesus*, 122–26.
11. Psalm 22:1 and Psalm 31:5 (cf. Matt. 27:46; Luke 23:46).
12. Matt. 4:17; Mark 1:15.
13. Matt. 21:28–32; Luke 15:7, 10.
14. Scripture testifies, ". . . nor was any deceit in his mouth" (Isa. 53:9)
    and "yet was without sin" (Heb. 4:15).
15. Matt. 9:15; Mark 2:20; Luke 5:35.

16. M. Robert Mulholland, *Invitation to a Journey: A Road Map for Spiritual Formation* (Downers Grove, IL: InterVarsity Press, 1993), 57.

17. Ibid., 58–73.

Experiencing God's Story

The Story Begins
The Authority of the Bible, the Triune God, the Great and Good God
978-0-8254-2595-0

The Hero Who Restores
Humanity, Satan and Sin, Jesus Christ
978-0-8254-2596-7

The Rescue
Salvation, the Holy Spirit, the Church
978-0-8254-2597-4

New People Forever
Transformation, Mission, the End
978-0-8254-2598-1

How do we conform to the image of Jesus Christ? How do we grow in maturity as believers? How do we truly live out and experience all that God is and all that He offers to us?

Designed to draw the participant into a deeper relationship with God, each of these four study guides probes three essential topics of spiritual formation. Presented through the three-step process of spiritual development—*believing*, *behaving*, and *becoming*—each topic examines a passage of Scripture, identifies and explains the theological principles of spiritual formation,' and offers personal application for continued spiritual growth.

J. Scott Duvall is professor of New Testament at Ouachita Baptist University, a liberal-arts Baptist college in Arkansas. He is coauthor of the popular *Grasping God's Word: A Hands-On Approach to Reading, Interpreting, and Applying the Bible.*

For more information, visit www.kregel.com/duvall.